To you, Bill,

for teaching me words,

words small, and words frugal,

but we make the most of them.

Descending song

I remember

       my days of vinegar.

Nowadays I just

        strum.

La di da

     di da dum

di da doo

      doo da da dum...

Oh hell, I've forgotten it, the melody in the

dream. The same they stood up and

applauded for, that same applause

I wanted to take, as a glove in my pocket,

from their to this world. But I remember nothing. Isn't that

just like dreams?

          But just let me sleep, I want to ask,

please, moon, find me sleeping beneath your light, please

don't draw teardrops below my eyes when I lay on my side,

please don't find me awake in the darkest hours. Please

let me close my eyes, and keep them closed.

             God help me

I'm so useless.

        Some music moves backward, I realized. Sometimes

a part takes your breath away, and you find a second hadn't passed,

so enormously moving it was. A song that wasn't in time.

I wouldn't mind writing one. But what use are songs

for those who no longer dream?

I used to sleep

to noon, sing songs, gaze at her

gazing at the sea. I couldn't call that a good life,

but it was a life. Now I'm just here, where strangers

paint their footsteps on the street, where leaves run in the wind,

where I hear laughter in the distance. To whom does this

laughter visit, where is the ear drawn

on the side of the face of the girl who laughs? I'm

just here, among the trees, like saccharide strangers,

these shadows like unwanted guests. I tell them I'm healing.

Now that's a laugh. I'm chained to my bed like an inmate.

How many hours must I lose before I am recovered?

and even if my soul were cured, I would

still be compelled to open the door, I would still be above

...above! this blue-tinged, rain-flattened earth.

I'm still here. They want me to stand up.

I'm beginning to think I should, too. But what

for? To accomplish dreams, to accomplish

ambitions? Is it that all I am are successes,

or the frustrations of? I'm not belief or faith, I'm

pus, I'm blood, I'm muscle, I'm shit,

I'm semen, I'm piss, but today, for this space,

I'm nothing, the nothing that is, the nothing that shall

be. I'm not different than she is,

I don't deserve to be anything else.

O

Orpheus singt! Everyone needs to know,

huh? Why don't you climb up the mountain

and your hands a horn tell it to the world

4

that I sing, of man's folly, my

stupidity, my inability and total lack

of desire to even get up?

Ecco Orfeo,

cui pur dianzi furon cibo i

sospir, bevanda il pianto. Rub it in,

why don't you. You want to make a picture

out of every tear, you want to tell me I had seen

worse days, but this, this is

the worst day, because you won't

shut up.

Ma, oh vano mio dolor!

I tell myself this every day, and yet grief

still doesn't let up. Go figure. I know now

how defective the human body is, nay,

how defective the human spirit is. I can yell

at myself, Get over it! a million times over,

a million times an hour, and reason goes

shallowly into the deepest plunges of my heart,

such that the only question is, Why

me?

The snotgreen sea. The scrotum

tightening sea. Epi oinopa ponton.

Sea whose horizons should contain hope,

let me sail over you, let me find her

again, her briny mind, her foaming thoughts,

her changing faces, like waves aroused by the wind.

You're the sea; come fill me in.

You're rainwater; wash me clean.

5

You're the tide; crash onto me.

You're wine; let me smell you.

You're light; shine on me.

You're light; let me see.

You're light.

Why must I grope through the dark?

You're light.

Why must I be denied warmth?

You're light.

Come to me, Eurydice, this night don't

evade me, don't slip from me, white thing,

for I know you are here, dancing on the floorboards, bare

foot, dancing to convince yourself you are real.

And

    Eurydice, you aren't dead. I

am. I and this world are dying,

its colors are fading, its objects have no joy,

even the sunlight despises it, it inspires nothing new,

it leaves behind ruins, baked red, left raw in the wind.

I'm the one whose dead, no other conclusion can

be, I'm a ghost, an empty thing, but a breath,

a dream flitting

to and fro

from this world to

the next, and the next one, how can I expect to live

very long? I can't make up my mind to descend

and see you again. I'm selfish, I know. When they

lowered you, they buried me too. Why couldn't they

bury the world too? What worth has the world?

Without you, isn't it a cheap thing? Eurydice,

6

you were treated like a cheap thing, and so being,

why can't I give it up also?

                              I just want you to

hear my voice just once, Eurydice, across the boundless

oceans of crying and always dying, I won't

tell you I love you, don't tell me

you're ok, just hear, goddamn you, hear the I

who spoke to you once, to the you you once were,

the you that I saw, the you that I sing about, the you

I'm forbidden to hold and yet each finger I can touch.

Eurydice, if it was yours to die, then why was mine

to remember everything about you?

I remember my days of vinegar. I remember my days of anger.

I remember how you fell. I remember that I felt

I should have followed you. I remember those days

of raging at the heavens, asking you too

must strike me with the lightning bolt, you

too must kill me, if you're not looking for enemies,

else answer yourself why you took the pains to make me,

for I will double that pain. Eurydice, I

fall too, let the whole world fall, let life fall,

from the top of this staircase, lower baluster and baluster,

let it crash on the tiling, let it shatter this

cheap, dollar-store thing, let death come,

                              O

loathsome death, cowardly, shrinking death, same as

took you away, companion of mine on this dark day,

death sitting on the moon, sitting sickly silvered,

his bloodsoaked hands arching over the werewolf trees,
the merchant iron, their tips like lances, held like
champions shouting and calling for the winds
to let the gashes of heaven bring rain down
from their wounds. Cut the world. A god can do it.
The rain paints the streets black, the rain cuts
the world with its slashing silver lines, the rain makes
bombast of the thunderclap. Eurydice,

                            I descend,

I descend not for your sake, I descend
as I have always done. I remember my descending, most
of all, the black smoke of hell, the noxious smell of
hell, because I am in hell, and I have never ascended
since the day I followed you. Let me be
a demon in my grief, or let me live
as something so ugly the world couldn't contain it,
for I have never lived until now. Love looks like Eurydice, but rage
most resembles me. Just ask God,
who created me to be complacent to him. Let
grief become ecstasy, let sorrow sour, finally,
into joy, let outrage be welcomed with open arms. Let
me descend.

                Eurydice, the days of vinegar are behind me.
But I remember them all the same. If you are
in this room with me, I am falling; please hold me.

Unrequited song

On the day you died

                    I did not love you.

When you said you wanted to die,

                           I said nothing.

I said, This is always you. You're always

like this. I think I said it. Or I stared

at the mirror, seeing myself, seeing you, waiting

for your storms to cease. I'm stormy too. Is that why we always find

ourselves in sympathy? I'm all rain too, like that afternoon

of the rain striking the roof, its white lines

etched on the window, or we were like that room

sealed away in the wet, apart from the world, if we left the door

we would walk in the wilds of the emptiness

our imagination conjures where it lacks. We were nothing in that room.

You knew that. You pouted, you threatened, you cried. But you did so to me,

who was nothing, and nothing responding is nothing doing.

It did not matter. We went to the reunion all the same,

that neither of us really wanted to go, we were going

only because we said we would, as if our

promises were woven into the thread of the universe, and if we pulled

one out, the universe would fall. We stood there limping,

our attire light, in the bedroom which was

the darkest of the apartment's, darker on this

dark day, hating each other, your black

hair falling onto the claw of your hand, up-pointed

as if holding the weapon of my destruction, your

black dress hiding your claws of attraction.

I did not love every of her, all the time, nor

all of her, some of the time, I did not

love some of her, all of the time, I did

not love her most of the time. I could sit

here and tell you, And yet I still loved her, and yet

we could have easily left the other, as we waited for the

train to arrive, her clutching her purse in the evening light,

her face fading in the evening light.

We don't even like parties. We don't even know

why we said yes. We don't even know why we

honor our commitments. We should be dishonest

people. But, nevertheless, we were

there, our hands on our mouths, our

hearts in our hands, not thinking, not saying

anything really, we were there, to bide the time,

we talked a lot, we laughed a lot, but we were barely

present, and when you stepped away, I didn't

want you then, I was thinking, this

is some great punch, in some party I don't want to be.

And that was the last I spoke to you. When I close my

eyes, I still see myself, holding that cup,

not caring where you went. When I close my eyes

I am not running to you, I am not asking you to stay,

I am pathetic with that cup and powerless

and I'm still not loving you.

I did not always love her, I treated her sometimes

as if she were barely there.

                  And yet I still loved her,

even though I knew so little about the stations of love.

I don't know how to love. This was frustrating to some.

I don't know how to love. Clearly, God had it out for me.

I don't know how to love. So I can't tell you if she loved me back.

In the

       wee hours of the night, I am not loving Eurydice.

In the

       hours when others sleep, I am walking around the apartment

thirty times, shuffling myself into sleep, seeing

the dogs of night, seeing who drives at this hour,

thinking of tomorrow, which is today, thinking

of the woman in the bedroom, and wishing

she were someone else, as punishment

for her unable to commiserate with my inability to

sleep, wishing I were transferred to another land

in another world in another life, thinking

how much more of a happiness it would be,

thinking how much of an albatross she is

on my neck, and finally seeing

myself make the last turn, and the last walk

up the steps, and ascending those stairs, thinking

of laying in bed with that immobile shape again.

Eurydice was an object

               to me.

We were simply there

             with the other.

11

We hardly did much. We would walk down
the road past the lake, saying nothing. In the
summer our hands were hot, in the winter
we put them in mittens, but in the spring
we held hands, swaying them gaily in the breeze
until they became sweaty, because that's what
we thought lovers did. We were hardly lovers, we
were more partners, in seeing neighborhood
kids, ice skaters, cars, seeing
the sun sink below the horizon, its
petals of light laid over the lake
like the embroidery of a glove, and when we
were tired we pushed ourselves into the train
and headed home, our dark home, where
the squeak of the floorboards was song enough,
and in the evening I made meals, in the evening
I put our clothes in the hamper, in the
evening I held her

                  and pressed my lips in her hair
while Netflix played softly in the background.
I thought I was loving her. I was not.
When she left

              I regretted all of these things,
because she left without knowing I loved her.

Eurydice did all the loving for me.
She made innumerable

                  patterns on the bed. I would wake with her feet
on my face. I would wake with hands on my stomach. I would wake
and she would be holding me. And her hair splayed on my face. Eurydice

12

would sleep to noon, grumble herself awake, shuffle to the bathroom,

and ask what we were doing. I said I don't know. Then we would drink

coffee. Then roam under a sheet of trees.

                              We wasted every day.

We threw our lives into the river, hoping they would flash back up. They

didn't. We were not sad to see them go beneath the emerald waters. It was ok

to go nowhere, to do nothing with it, life, I mean, it was ok

we were a lot of afternoons to sift through before we redeemed our lives.

Eurydice told me

                    she loved me. She told me

after phone calls, when she walked out the door, when

I bought her things for Valentine's day, when I

bought her things for her birthday, when we

were traveling far from one another, family holidays

between us, after we watched movies that

upset her greatly, and whenever she felt like it,

whenever it was winter essentially, the days when she got

real sad, days when she didn't want to leave the bed,

white plain, where she complained she had a migraine,

and asked me for water all times of the day.

And I never told her, I love you, back,

I thought men shouldn't say I love you

so innocently and immoderately, and I always

thought, What a silly thing you are, Eurydice,

for so casually and ineffectually telling someone

so dire a statement as I love you.

I kept my heart closed. I closed my heart

                              in a book.

13

I spent so many hours reading

                     a book.

I have spent so many hours in this chair,

whose arms she sat on (she preferred the left,

closest to the doorway) and asked me questions I

ignored by burying my nose and my sight

in a book. I have spent so many hours ignoring

her by reading aloud the sentences in a book.

I thought I was educating myself, teaching

myself about the world, covering over

the inadequacies of myself and Eurydice, making

myself smarter, and therefore a better

lover to Eurydice, by finding the lover I

could be in a book, or in a song,

as if after so many periods and pauses

I would step on a mountain and see my surroundings

entire. I thought the world was little;

I thought I could have it, because I had so

little, because I had Eurydice and her

dating shows, bad pasta, her little

politics, her disrespect for my reading time.

Clearly, there was little in her.

                         I seek now

myself in these books, and see nothing in

them, and ask myself, What did you find?

I have burned my books entire.

I have ripped to shreds my writing,

these doggrels, meager, meaning

nothing, I thought they were something, before

14

I lost her, not that Eurydice is

meaning, but that there is no meaning.

Meaning is a lot of fire and a lot of smoke

and a lot of ashes and a lot of me losing

my hair, and looking like a fool,

because I am looking at these ashes

thinking they're the ashes of love. Would she

have been touched by these totems of affection?

Should I tell her

     they're not for her,

they're for me, to let me know I'm still alive?

I am stepping out

    of a book.

I can pile and pile on words,

       I can

mount more and more commas, until

it won't do me any good, I know I fucked up,

I know too late what love is. We were

of a kind. I know that from looking

at other lovers, when I was not looking at her.

We were neither good nor bad, we found ourselves

in pubs, in parks, in malls, in museums,

in dancehalls, in banquets, in bookstores, in

arcades, in plazas, in pizzerias, in

promenades, in squares, in saunas, in cemetaries,

in supermarkets, in pharmacies, in dorm rooms, in zoos,

in creameries, in cafés, in haunted houses,

we were always unwilling participants, and we were always winding through

staircases and hallways for bathrooms, and we were always

guests in a stranger's eyes, without tickets or passports, and she would ask me, In the maelstrom, would you find me?

And I never answered yes,

                                  but I didn't say no.

I don't know how to love, I can't love, I don't love.

I won't love.

                    I can blame everyone, I can blame

my father who hurt my mother, I can blame my mother

for overindulging me, I can blame my siblings for being selfish,

I can blame this world which confuses love

for commodity, I can blame God for making me

impossible, and I would still blame myself at the end.

                                                  I wish

I never sought her. I wish we never met. I wish we

hadn't met in the rain, our umbrellas up, hardly hearing

the other in the gunfire, happy all the same, the lamp

slopping pools of light on our faces, where she

hid a smile, that danced in her eyes.

                              I wish I

never thought she was cute, never thought she was smart,

never thought she was good-looking, never thought we

clicked, never thought I could take care of

her, and never forgave her, never defended

her, never coddled her, never argued

with her, never had sex with her,

never got angry with her, never asked her

to pay the phone bill, never put her name

on the lease, I merely wanted to live

with her, I merely wanted her beside

me, I just wanted to love her

so I could come to love myself.

                    Eurydice,

we held hands

            we lashed arms

                    braided our legs

pressed our lips

            folded our bellies

                    our cheeks

brushing,

            and, releasing, tumbled upon the other,

                                    but I

just wanted you to hold me

                in front of the stars.

And, did I hold her in return?

I'm sorry

        for not having held you.

I'm sorry

        for being absent.

I'm sorry for not being the one you wanted.

I'm sorry there wasn't a happier way out.

                                And, I'm sorry

this comes too late. That it took me this long

to come to any understanding of you, that

words fail to describe you, and words fail

to make me more satisfied of you. Eurydice,

you were you, you're a warmth in a cold

earth, you're a luminosity in a dark

world, you're a blade of grass on an empty

plain, because you were, nothing else, and death

17

took that away from you, and took from me my

seeing you as you truly were. The words

never come out right, I always misinterpreted

you, and I'm doomed to apologize to you forever

and an eternity more seek my way out of

forgiveness because I haven't made up my mind.

Eurydice, I am

        descending

           to find myself again

and if I don't, then I know

           this life

wasn't made for me. Eurydice, you fell

so I could fall.

        So fall for me,

once more, Eurydice, fall

           so I may come up whole.

Folly song

I don't want to die. But I count myself among the dead
for I, too, am spiralling down life,

which is a stairwell
through which so many souls climb down, skiffs
on the dark waters, white sails unfurled, towards their
destination, their final death. For, you see, one must live many lives,
and die in them all, before exiting consequence, or so they told me.

Eurydice, I'm coming to you

on the backs of the dead.
I am stepping on the backs of the dead, to come to you.
You would blush to know so. But "the descent
to hell is the same from every place." Now who said that?
Laërtius? No, William Gass, quoting Laërtius.
When Diogenes said it, he said, Anaxagoras says;
but himself said it, so held in his voice, so Laërtius says,
holding Anaxagoras, so said, saying Anaxagoras,
not the other way around. For the song is the singer.
When Anaxagoras said it, he meant something beautiful;
when Laërtius said it, he discovered it scandalous;
when Bill said it, he wanted to make something ugly
out of something beautiful. It's a mean thing
to reuse someone else's words, but the world is
a mean thing, and our ways are so crooked, and our
orientation so inverted, that we can believe out of
cruelty something good may come. What insanity.

19

But that was Bill's point: we're insane. We're
full of shit. We're dying. We won't be missed.

Bill, be my muse, reluctant though you are. You're
a fat angel, without wings, for you haven't earned any.
You must loathe Clarence Oddbody. You must hate
Capra's Wonderful Life, film full of dreck, despise
that an angel earns their wings contingent
on hearing a bell ring. Why a bell? Smart ass, you
say, why not a trumpet, as blown at Jericho,
why not a drum, pa rum pa pa pum, why
an auditory cue, why not red lightning streaked
across the sky, for God, Jewy God, prefers
wrath over mercy, and would rather dress his assistants
in martial decor, than with something so bland
as a fucking bell? Well, get your wings today.
Inspire me with song, enough rope, to climb down.
Sing me your song
                    of drunks, of ingrates,
of losers, of gamblers, of wife beaters,
miserly men, apes, fascists of the heart, lions
in their minds only. That's who hell is full of,
so we're told. Bill,
                    I have come to hate you,
you piece of shit. How long have we been acquainted?
Since eighteen? Congratulations, you're barely a
pedarast. Must make you so happy. Did you think
frigging boys was akin to playing muse,
did you imagine yourself Plato? God, you all
are a sick lot, you fucking writers, writing,

20

shaming, nagging the human race to follow your ways.

Picture me, in the flush of my youth, green and

white-hearted, reading you, wanting to write like

you, my ass the same shape as yours, having

sat so long, believing beauty resides in a good

book, and now we resent each other. Head full of book,

that's no way to live a life. And I learned that

reading every book. Browne, Broch, Browning,

don't these writers realize their books

stink of dying and yet they write lives

and lines longer than the count of lives themselves

and look feeble for it, and only prove

we are running from life itself, we leap into the arms

of death. There are more words written than people.

There are more characters than letters. They say

there are worlds in books. Fuck no. There are only people

in books, frail, mortal, some fat like you,

Bill, and they disguise their gluttony and minor sins

as heroic. Bill. I hate writing,

I hate writers, I hate readers, I hate sickness

and disease, and all they entail, which is death,

and I hate those who fetishize death.

I have written myself into a labyrinth, and I can't

get out. I don't know what is human in this dark.

Bill, hell is all you ever wanted. At least I

learned that. You wanted to know how hot hell

was, you wanted to know the needles devils prick

you with, you wanted to know what it was like,

so you could slide down as quickly, because

you hated life too, and you couldn't conceive

anything worse after. Bill, I'm not afraid

any longer of seeing every sin, of knowing

every evil I'll do, I know now

I'll do them all anyway. Bill,

we're hardly human. Bill, we can go

down

      easy. Be my Virgil. I'll play you Dante.

We'll pretend

              we're peeking at naked girls for honesty,

we're watching popes burn in coffins for sincerity,

we're watching them shit themselves for penitence,

when really we watch because we're hateful, and

implicate ourselves. This is the true

divine comedy, for we know we too

will be fucked in the ass as they, who were once

handsome and tall as you.

ABANDON ALL HOPE, YE WHO ENTER.

"I summon to the winding ancient stair,

set all your mind upon the steep ascent,

upon the broken, crumbling battlement,

upon the breathless starlit air." Yeats,

you saw so much in your life, you saw

second comings, you saw men crumple,

you saw the wreck and ruin of civilization,

you saw love unreturned, you saw

the disgrace of age, you saw the staircase

as clearly as I do and you ascribed it to heaven

while mine winds down to hell, all on a

22

politician's pension. But heaven and hell

are one and the same, as hope is a delusion,

despair is also, hope is as complicit

to our suffering as the heart is.

Spinoza said so. Once you stop hoping

the clouds clear, the celestial machine shines,

and you begin living, as in, you start your dying,

your final and true destination.

A passage is a staircase down into hell.

A stanza, a step. A writer writes so many

because hell is made of so many. Leonard said

Hank Williams was a hundred floors above, err,

below him, Hank who sang "You'll walk the floor

the way I do." You live all life

to prepare for hell. You live through

ungrateful girlfriends, dollar days, albatrosses

round necks, complicated games, growing older.

You never become numb to suffering,

to black boys with bulging bellies, to dogs

minced into meat, to car crashes, to

divorce, to ingratitude, and finally

the paralyzing dark of our limbs

                              shutting off,

with nothing else to remember us by.

Day by day you slowly lose out hope

that this world is redeemable, but never that

tomorrow, we can go down lower still.

We build hell in our heads every day

until it's boring, and yet tomorrow start anew

23

because in creating hell we become godlike,

we become individual, we become unique, we become

ourselves, and answer only to our actions.

Hell is but the world without its blemishes.

What blushing boy in us denies this?

In hate we are human. In hate we relate

to a hateful earth. In hate we derive from God

who hates us. Heaven has to be a going down,

for our hearts are deep undertakings.

Now, boatman Charon, dip down your

oar into holy waters, sing up the

fisherman's song on the waves of

Acheron, angling the ungrateful,

the refusers, the cowards, the

slow-in-deliberating, the

salarymen, the drunkards, the couch

potatoes, the bookworms, the bad in

bed, the Sunday shoppers, the performance

artists, the knitters, the bed

wetters, the bloggers, the teacher's

pets, the pornographers, the professors,

the waiters, the manicurists, the

dog sitters, the gardeners, the carpenters,

the chronically ill, the early birds,

the incontinent, the dilly-dalliers, every

one who merely wished to sail all their

lives on comfortable waters and do nothing, only

to spill into the swamp of their do-nothing.

Charon, "the lives of the wealthy are one long

Sunday," but even you know this is half-truth.

You don't need much to waste your life. You merely

pick up your hand,

                    cover your eyes, kick

your head back, and, in the darkness,

                                        drown.

And I wish I did

                a lot less listening

for then I wouldn't have

                    lived my life in so much

fear I wasn't living a good one

                    indeed, I lived

a bad one

            when all of life, is a life,

                            all we do, is folly.

I remember distinctly the day of my fear. I was

asked if I believed in God. I felt, if I answered

No, I would be admitting living was a long con game,

that to live was to hope, one day, you'll be lucky

and be happy. I sought thereon

                            the works of Plato, who

spoke so clearly and strongly during his trial,

                            who spent

his life reading the images in the water, so as

to make out their true meaning and

                            compared our lives

to flickering shadows, against the backdrop of a burning sun.

I loved Plato. Through him, I understood words clear.

Through him, I started sparks

                              of intelligence in my mind,
found I could think surely and confidently, and felt
I could know something about the world.

                              But the dark
in one's heart

                    is all devouring. I thought I found
myself kindred with Aristotle, who asserted virtue was
a kind of action, that the man of most strength was he
who refrained. I thought I tapped into veins deep
by taking Confucius' "To say you know when you
know, and to say you do not know when you do not,
that is knowledge," and accepted his axiom:
death has always been with us. I found Zhuangzi's belief
that it is better to live life as a useless tree, and to
not concern ourselves with this or that, with the color
blue or red, or the color good or bad, and to simply be,
poignant. Then there's Nietzche's jubilation in exclaiming,
God is dead, and that we must answer to ourselves, and Spinoza's
God is substance, in which we partake of, and to live itself
a privilege and an honor, to become god-like in our joy;
I thought these were welcomed by the Tao, and Guanyin's sense
that this life is but a moon on the waters, and these
little sufferings and little hopes are but blossoms in the wind.
Browne's "Time hath endless rarities, and shows
of all varieties; which reveals old things in heaven,
makes new discoveries in earth"; Montaigne's "I
am little subject to the passions. My susceptibility
is naturally tough; and I harden and thicken it every
day by force of reason"; and Smith's ideal
that two greyhounds act in accord for the object of their

26

desire, though they communicate not; I believed

we always strive to be our better, for a little while. And

something appeals to me concerning Whitman's "I celebrate

myself" and Thoreau's search for wildness, and Diogenes'

"I bite my friends, to save them." And, Bill, you said

nothing keeps the sadness away like a book. But this is all

                                        for naught.

For I still feel fear.

                     I fear only the ignorant are rewarded,

I fear there is no righteousness in hard working,

                                    I fear

children will grow hateful, and spiteful,

                          I fear the kind

are but so many pebbles for the unjust to walk over,

I fear we were all put here just to suffer.

                             I fear all.

And I fear most, I will go to my grave in silence, knowing all.

Pallas, why do you hold your aegis down?

the same shield that by acts of virtue

Perseus consecrated, that with fearsome

roarings shook Mount Ida once,

that made men hesitate from using their fists,

made men tremble and humble in their

mortality, long-living once the

precious, true and worthy object of war?

Pallas, I suspect you don't flock the heavens.

Pallas, I fear you don't have the power

to forebear my entry into the cookie jar.

Pallas, I think you are an object of

sex for hoary-headed men who have

spent all of their lives confined to their desks

learning the ways of man to learn nothing

to masturbate upon in the unfound hope of a heaven

where girls simply love them for their virtue

and virtue only.

            Pallas, I think we live in a world

hating justice. I think we live in a world

every man wants to remake in their image.

I think we live in a world where men lie so much

because they feel the insanity of this world is a lie

and their lie is better than the one we were born on.

Sometimes I feel

            I am fundamentally alone

                      in this world and

the denizens of this world

            only exist to see

                  how far I can

go before I decide to end myself, as would be sensible.

I wish everyone would just shut the fuck up. I wish

people wouldn't be so stupid. I wish Plato one day

would reason with the little doing and little knowing in man

millenia after his work was written. There are no minds

to ennoble. There is no hope for peace. There is no virtue

to foster. We are animals made to screw and kill our neighbors

so as to have our slight chance of survival

                and then

to disappear into the dust the earth was always made of.

I used to believe so much in the Bible. I believed in Christ's

This is the god of the living, not of the dead, that the Lord is the god of trueth and righteousness, in Elijah's

The Lord was not in the wind, but now I believe

$$in\ nothing.$$

There is no god. I cannot conceive an intelligence who so hates

everything he has created, and I cannot imagine a creator

who so hates me. I believe in Broch's, I am bleeding, with:

Yes, you are. If any philosopher suits me, it's Wittgenstein:

Whereof we cannot speak, thereof one must be silent. Yet even

that is too much wind. Life is Zeno holding his breath, blue-

faced, after quoting, "I come, I come, why dost thou call for me?"

I see now Minos does so little, like every

sinecured judge, when man is

so sufficient in implicating himself

in all the evils he has done to himself,

every defect he has added to himself, every

injury he has caused, and the powerlessness

he has engendered; and Minos yawns, stretches

his tail, and lets each sufferer go

$$to\ the\ damning\ of\ his\ own\ choosing.$$

It's a shame I rejected God so late

$$for\ I\ love\ me\ a\ lot\ to\ masturbate.$$

I spent many hours

$$stroking\ myself$$

$$in\ bed\ or\ on\ the\ couch$$

surprised by the sudden seizure of

$$desire\ building\ into\ climax$$

releasing it all

$$into\ the\ tiny\ lake$$

                    my belly button is

and then stared at the ceiling lights, my body complete, letting

the jets of love make rivers.

                         "And if any man's seed of copulation

go out from him, then he shall wash all his flesh in water,

and be unclean until the even."

                    I'd stare down the drain

my seed fell into,

          feel my soul go down

                         with it.

When I was a kid, I pat it down with a blanket.

It's odd this little organ can stimulate more belief

than the brain can. Masturbation is a kind of hiding

yourself. It's a bludgeoning of the world that is and

the world in your mind. It's not so with so many other

sins. You can't pretend to be rich. You can't pretend

to be mad. But you can pretend you're entering

a beautiful woman, and in the tangles of her hair pretend

she loves you actually.

              I can make her now,

I can see her now, within these hands I can mold

her now, a woman who will hold me in

careful consideration and who will understand me through

sad and soft spells and who will love me as a mother loves her

child and who has eyes for me and only me, my dear

Ramona, my hands are the shape of your breasts, my hands

are the shape of your hips, Ramona, my hands excite heat

underneath your skin, Ramona, I relieve my thirst by means

of your lips, Ramona, I rove between the falls

                    30

of your hair, to plant kisses on the nape of your neck,

Ramona, your cunt is not a hole, it is a space I so lack

and wish to live in. It's plain to see men are ill-equipped

for sexuality. We crave to drink the waters of women.

Let loose yourself on my tongue, Ramona, I want to feel your

flows between my legs, oh Ramona, why can't you speak

to me and fill me in with your breath, Ramona, you're all

I need, so it stands that I should be all you need, poor

as I am. Isn't that a fair trade, that I'm all the brains you need?

Ramona, lower your mouth

and let your waters rejuvenate me.

Which of the women in my collection shall you become?

I pretended

to love Colette. I pretended to love a woman for her mind.

And Colette allowed everything into hers. I want to be beside her

as she hears "the snow whisper on the bed of dead leaves", which sounds

like "the quiet praying of a crowd at worship."

This same girl who "reveled in being a Plain Jane, with

my hair in pigtails and straight wisps straggling over

my cheeks", would later with amazing recall recount

that "the last five steps each gave out their particular

note like a xylophone – B, B flat, C, D, and then dropping

a fifth to G" in her days of the revue.

Colette's lights

are "so white they are mauve" and "sting

to the point of tears." A baby is a "fair chubby-cheeked

Eros." Her boys ride clouds of lavender as if they're horses.

Colettevilli, I want to live in your world

of hungry girls

31

in the revue, damsels locked all days in rooms,

middle-aged women stung by loneliness, of men seized

by the bridles of love and unable to let go of their temptations,

of lovers suddenly turned cold, or partners turning away -

I want to live in the world that you thought was beautiful to live in,

I want to live in the Thousand and One Nights, where the pattern

of a scarf or napkin enraptured you, that same where the boughs

of trees and the tender vine were curled around your finger,

the same world where the sea made love to the shore in warm waves,

that same where memory is sweet, for in every one you are alive in it.

I pretended to love

        Katherine Anne Porter

                whose

strength I sought a piece of. She and I shared the doubt

that life was a bag of disappointments. We "examined

the objects, one by one, and did not find them in themselves

impressive." A realist, for my heart. For in frolicking in reality,

Kate sought a better and true world.

                "They seemed

to have no place in the world."

            And so you went down

to Mexico, those days of finding buckshot

through hospital windows, of revolutionaries

waving rifles and the red and green flag,

days of hoarse, rapid-fire Spanish, until

you became disillusioned that these men,

too, were playing tyrant, just like the boys in

olive drab back home, playing with the guns

their toys had in hand in someone else's fool war.

Even in those hotblooded days you knew man's
beauty laid in the stock he set on justice
and not the guts he spilled on the battlefield.

Kate, let me look into the
agate of your eyes, that same steely gaze
that saw so many assaults on time, that saw
the deaths of so many children, and lovers
become spiteful and lovers become disappointing.
Kate, you just wanted someone to care about you
through the Spanish Flu. Is the cure for loneliness
for you also a drop in the dried wells of love?
Kate, did you want the kindness of someone
who would withstand the indignities of life
with you?
              "Don't you love being alive? Don't
you love weather and the colors of different times
of the day, and all the sounds and voices like children
screaming in the next lot, and automobile horns and
little bands playing in the street and the smell
of food cooking?" "Adam, I love you, and I was
hoping you would say that to me, too."

I pretended to love
              Marianne Moore
                            who said of her
prize bird, "You suit me well, for you can make
me laugh, nor are you blinded by the chaff
that every wind leads spinning from the rick."
Your mind was an "enchanted thing", "like the

glaze on a katydid wing,

                subdivided by sun,

till the nettings are legion."

                Marianne, has anyone

said this to you: You're impossibly cute?

I love that you say, "Genesis tells us of Jubal and

Jabal.

      One handled the harp and one herded the cattle."

Your nautilus "knew love

              is the only fortress

strong enough to trust to." Your pelican

"finds sticks for the swan's-down-dress

of his child to rest upon and would

             not know

Gretel from Hänsel." Of men, you said:

"Men are monopolists

           of 'stars, garters, buttons

and other shining baubles' -

          unfit to be the

guardians of another person's happiness."

I do

   want to

      love you, Marianne. I had always

thought there was a cruelty in knowledge, but you

are the louvre through which I know knowledge

is light. A fact is a sweet taste for the mind

because it says something about that mind which

but born is all flavorless black. To learn is to find

something new,

      and to be new, in a dying world.

34

It's not languishing in this chair, which is all I've

ever done.

        Marianne,

                I want to roam through the

curls on your head,

             find in them the spaces and the

silences you put between your words,

                        find in them

the rhythm, holy rhythm, that pitter-patter

through your soul,

           find in them a reason to

live on in this decaying world, and for you.

You're the moonlight on the bed, making a curtain

on the linen, and I'm the window letting you in.

Ramona, I never noticed how fair your skin was

until illuminated in the moonlight. Come to me now,

out of the dark, come into my hands, where I hold

your hair in the cups of my hands, where your face, where

your lips are drawn like footsteps, is directed to my face,

where your eyes are like water, lambent under the twilight,

Ramona – as much as I want to be beside you, as much as I

want to pick up the strands of your hair straggling

the bedside, I'm leaving,

                   our bodies are falling apart,

our sight is departing, and we don't look at the other the same

as we did when we felt the first rages of lust. Ramona,

consideration falls apart too, we stop looking at the other

like objects, we see the other as human,

                        and the humanity we hate

in ourselves we hate in the other. Ramona, that's all love is:

the object of love is to see in our love an object,

something we play with in hopes we become what

we pretend. And then we grow up. I wish you stayed

in your block of marble. But it's too late,

                              we're

fragmenting,

           the lashes of love can't hold everything

together,

      indeed these ribbons

                fall with us also

                      so that

we're but

      earth and string at the end. And, Ramona,

block of stone that once was my love, it's your

fault, for all this. You shouldn't have loved me,

you really are just a space for the winds of love

to occupy. Your cunt is a place for children to come out of

and for men to place their pain in. It's your fault for being

so vulnerable. And it's mine for talking to lumps of clay.

Big breasted.

      Big ass.

          Tanlines.

             Gym

shorts.

    Swimsuit.

        Czech.

        Tattooed.

Ponytail.

Anal.

Footjob.

Office.

Demure.

Gigi.

Noon Wine.

Like a Bulwark.

Court and Spark.

Women are so many kisses to men,

women are

so many words for men to justify.

We're fooling ourselves

if we believe lust pupates into love. Love? Who doesn't put

a premium on affection?

I'll go downward to the pools

of myself, enter the valleys of my loneliness, hear the wind

raking the blood in my brain, trace with my feet the looming

shadows of the crags, I'll deny myself, and meditate on

the meaning of love, unconfused with lust, find the necessity

in women, finding the necessity in myself, in my solitude

find the woman I always want to be with, for all life.

Oh, now I get it.

I want someone who is exactly like me.

No wonder people think

I'm gay.

Aristophanes said

man and woman are halves of a whole. But men are

narcissists, we're slow to admit what it is we lack.

Love cannot be unconditional. Not when our existence

is contingent. Not when our needs are mortal.

Not when through our eyes enters the image of beauty,

and by beauty, we distinguish, dissect and divide.

To live is to live violently.

How can I be expected to love

                              when I little love myself;

and I can't come to love myself

                              because, who could love me?

Here is your bride, here is your groom.

Both of their brows are pent up with doom.

They both fear what the Fates spell on their looms,

and they both fear a lifetime of the other's fart fumes.

And everyone else is pleased, except they,

everyone else is pleased by the wine but they,

today they are normal, tomorrow, behind

closed doors they rage and rake the other's eyes,

but today, at least, today they are normal.

I just want to be a normal human being for once,

with normal feelings, with a normal outlook on life,

with a normal amount of joy, with a normal future

as befits a normal earth having progressed normally,

where everyone before and after were and will be normal.

Why can't I just get this one simple fucking thing right?

That of loving another as my body yearns to.

When you're young you see

                              lots of images

of boys and girls loving one another, and in your heart

you feel the contentedness that comes from being

so pleasing in another person's eyes, and when you sleep

you think fondly, then fall asleep, then dream fondly

on these images, spread out warmly on your side,

so that when you are older lying awake

in the cold studio room, you hold out your arms

to warm yourself, because the one you dreamt

to be holding you keeping you warm, isn't there.

Now, is this thing real, or is it made up,

but if unreal, who is capable of making it up?

I'm accustomed to being on my lonesome

                                because I'm accustomed

to being loathed.

                I spent so many days rolling up hills,

surveying all I saw, master of it all, for one truly is a master

of one's sight. "I believe all I'm told, I've disbelieved only

too much in my long life, now I swallow everything, greedily."

In my sight I swallow the smokestacks billowing from the

chimneys, pushing out and growing bigger and becoming hazier in the

cold air, an analogy to my breath, which obscures my

glasses, and lingers on window panes, and an analogy to

me, who bundled myself up and made myself large to go out

so I wouldn't be alone. And downhill men in their parkas

are buying their daughters' prescriptions, down hill waiters

are running to and from banks, downhill students

are loitering at the Dunkin', downhill a grandmother

watches on her walker. Everyone has their place in the world but me. Downstream the green, turgid waters enter the bend,

downstream are some dead trees, downstream are the ducks

of summer just trying to make it to spring. The bridge beneath

made of brick and mortar sags under the weight

of so many other souls in the past, some here in hell.

If I'm quiet, I can hear them living, in the whistle

of geese as they fly through the empty expanses of

air which are silent here, silenter everywhere else.

And, as is routine, I peer inside the Chinese restaurant

hoping to find myself in it, for I so long to taste

orange chicken. No luck. The clerk is bored,

is scratching her wrist, is hidden behind a

breastwork of paper bags, awaiting their holders.

I'm

    downtown amid the brownstones and I'm moving

mouthfuls of chicken down a black spork and I'm

watching every coat pass me by, they're white and puffy,

black and woolen, goose down, crinkled, tan buttoned,

feathered, zipped, segmented like Mongolian armor,

holding the lives carried through the cobblestones of the alley.

I'm

    singing "T.V. Eye"

                    traversing

the long bridge over the Charles

                         frozen over,

those roaring breakers,

                    those waves, once white-foamed,

and even the rills

that spill into the damp earth

are stopped

in their place,

sculptured,

set apart from time,

as if their anger stops

even in this cold

where my hands clutch my heart for warmth,

so I expect even hell to freeze someday,

and even the sadness in that heart.

And when I'm so cold, I become numb all over
and my balls shrink into my body, I yell Iggy's LORD
hoping it resonates in the vaults of me, that I'm
still alive, and I can be angry still.

I'm watching other people live their lives.

"She's got a T.V. eye

on me." It's other people

who have birthdays, who celebrate holidays,

who have weddings, who have friends, who converse, who
accumulate hobbies, who see things through, who eat out
at restaurants, who share experiences, who laugh at others'
jokes, who are interesting, who remember joys with other people
while I remember only the details of myself. And yet in all this
I still long for peoples' presences and go out in spite of my pain.

And sometimes they conspire, the wind conspires, and I know
that I'm an impossible ugly thing.

I'm

    climbing down the dusty boulevard, I have spent
so many days

                 waiting before crosswalks, looking left
and right for cars before I cut the street, lest they cut me,
staring at someone's head – staring at their curls, staring
at their weave, bob, ponytail, their pins, clips, their
pate, two strips of hair, their braid, their dome -
before wordlessly and a little impudently cutting ahead of them
letting them see the tail of my coat.

                  I'm listening

                        to the clicks
of traffic lights, the hum of motors, the pigeons coo-coo,
the vroom of minivans, children buh-byeing, basketballs
pounding on pavement, footsteps, a choir of dogs,
and, though it is denied, the whisper of the wind
above my head, lightly past my ear, for the wind does
talk to you.

      I'm

        sipping iced

           tea

              and nibbling on a
chicken sandwich, preserving bites to make it last,
to make the moment last, while peering beneath
the poster to see people's feet – to see sneakers,
laced-up boots, sandals, pumps, stilettos, Crocs,
flats, brogues – just to see movement, to see light.

And as the LEDs of Times Square lapse into
the lamps of Central Park, I ask

                    where, indeed,
did the time go? Where did my life go?

I'm
    climbing up the branch-shaded, pebble-strewn paths
of the Hradčany,
                I'm huffing and heaving on the hills
of Seattle,
                I'm surveying the clouds in the canals of
Amsterdam,
                I'm looking down the lifeless avenues of
Fort Lauderdale.
                "Blessed rage for order,
                            pale Ramon."
And in Chicago I'm bare-armed amid the white sails,
and in D.C. moss floats on the reflecting pool.

"I don't so love blossoms I want to die. I'm afraid
once they are gone of old age still more impetuous."

And in the left wing of the museum I saw
the chipped and gold-faded semblance of Guanyin
a hand on her knee and a hand to the earth
staring at the waters where the moon blossoms like
a flower and she knows the flower is not real
despite how beautiful it is and how much she loves life.

What, shall I go me to Machu Picchu,
shall I go me to the Grand Canyon,
shall I go to Hawaii, or Barcelona,

43

shall I go to Tokyo, or Berlin,

or should I go to Gaza and Syria,

or where the Uighurs are dying,

where the Poles had died, or where

the Serbs still suffer today?

All these little bites in sight

                                     are boorish appetites.

Does the cruel earth remember our footsteps? Does it memorialize its bodies?

Sometimes I feel I am the only person who is real.

And where are you, in all this? You should be here

in the Sears, you should be here in Saks, you should

be here in the park with me, under the reeds, observing

the lake, kicking up dust, feeding the swans, you should be

here in the McDonald's, on the dirty, smudgy tiles of the

McDonald's, whose mud are so many remainders of a

rainy city, whose humidity is french fry steam, whose dance

are the aprons of the tired workers, eager to head home

this drizzly day, you should be here on the length of Fifth Avenue,

look, snow is falling on people's hats, on people's hair

as they jostle and fight to see the Christmas tree, and we

laugh at them – as we had once, as in our younger bodies,

and we were young once, and poor, as we laughed through the city,

as we laughed in the hallways that were more a home

than the homes we solemnly returned to as the dusk bleeds

the horizon, and made a home, one in the other, we were

believing happiness were things never changing between

us.

And now I'm here.

And it's my fault.

And we
were always jumping in and out of cars, and we were
always writing homework on the dirty floor, and we
were always visiting the other just to say hello.
And where are we now?

Happiness is me being
with you forever. So where are we now? Ah,
that's it – nothing lasts forever.

And we
are arguing – I don't recall what – you
want to fight, fine, let's fight – I'm always
fighting, who isn't fighting for their tiny
space in this life, fighting for this small
scrap of living deigned to us – and I'm always
arguing, sure, I think I'm always right, but why
am I always arguing with you, it's not like
we're fucking or anything – and yet, it doesn't
matter what we're arguing about, what we're
fighting over is, is this really the moment we
believe it is, the falling-out that we felt could
happen –

and it is.

And it's my fault.
We're just bites. Befriending is just biting
a mouthful of another person until you're full
and finding yourself on a balcony of stars
wondering where that same hunger went.

45

And living is death biting us and being pleased by it.

And befriending is seeing your old friends you have grown
out of in another person's body, and befriending is
belittling your intelligence and believing that one can run
eternal. Befriending is believing you won't be alone.

I'm alone, alone. A teacher taught me the word
alone. I didn't think it would happen to me,
but I find the word is a curse, from my primordial
origins. The word chases me from the dark and to
the dark, saying, you shall be alone, alone.
I can blame myself all I want but it won't change
the fact: when the sky colors dark and
another day is wasted, it hurts the most.

And the mallards run around the pond
and the mallards nibble on dandelions
and the mallards leave behind rolled dung
and the mallards fly north when the lake freezes.

And why do I remember these memories specifically
and I'm cursed to remember no others?

These memories are all I have, of a life that seems
plausible, and yet my pain lies in their plausibility.

"Memory,

　　　　turn your face to the moonlight."

Memory, forgive me for all my sins,

memory, find me in the morning without guilt,

memory, don't let me curse myself anymore,

memory, give me from my memories a reason to live.

Memory, why is it that you resemble nothing like

a photo album and more like the crystallized dew

of the moonlight which turns into mist the moment

they feel the warmth of our fingertips? Is it because

memories are meant to be unkind, or memories are meant

to be fragile, so we're more willing to live in reality,

or is it to remind us that we're always in our night?

The cat cries in the morning. He wants to be let in.

Birds are on the sill. I wordlessly open the door.

He climbs up the cabinets, startling them to flight.

And one stays behind. There is a glass pane

between him and his appetite. Does he know this?

"Every morning, when I woke, the world appeared grayer

and I didn't notice because everything remained

in the same palette; and in that day there wasn't a

brushstroke of the color of the day before."

One could hear the water trickling

                              as Colette heard

on the day of her wedding. The water ran through the rows

the Mexicans drew in the mud with their hoes. The lamps

were wrapped in mist, which the spring had melted

of the snow from a winter come too late. The sky is a

Spanish blue, to which the worms hail and scratch their heads.

Tomorrow the grass will come up tough, tall and hale.

I'm in the lecture hall, alone, reading Zvevo, reading

these lines at a cramped chair whose desk doesn't fully

lower. And I feel old. I have seen all time.

I had barely left my teens and I saw the shade of my

mortality. Death finally is being bored of everything.

There's nothing new in this earth,

                                          we just pretend we're new.

Everthing on it was invented at once.

                                         When we were born, we knew that.

We try to discover the reasons

                                     to keep shuffling our corpses around.

I know what my grandmother is doing today. In the

biting morning cold she is wrapping herself in scarf and mitts

and walking around the neighborhood. She makes small talk

with a local woman, they discuss their grandchildren, me, the

casino, TV, then let the wind fall in the gaps of their silence

installed into their brains, returning to their grandchildren again.

She then slowly climbs up the steps to her apartment, watches TV,

eats two further meals, and then sleeps, after a flurry of calls

to her brood.

                    In Guangdong, in Santo Domingo, in New

York, it all ends the same: here on her La-Z-Boy watching

Taiwanese films,

                    and her asking me to fix the television, in whiles.

What does it matter? No matter what I do,

good or ill, I live on. What reward?

I was born an old man, with woman's breasts.

I have seen into the future; it is barren.

There is some rust when I close my hand;

there is a stab in my back, when I stand up;

there is an ache in my stomach, when I sit down;

and now my sight, the horizon is eating more of it.

I see it all. I live it all again. The ruins

of a home, a lot choked with weeds, the gutter

where so many pigeons have died. On these long and dusty

streets, beaten by martial feet, I thirst

for a voice – you hear a lot of stories,

especially with your eyes closed. You hear a lot

of resentments, of closet infidelities, families feuding,

drug deals, begging, recommendations to God, gunshots

and footfalls and ambulance sirens, and the complaints

of the deaf and impotent scattered like seeds into

the wind in the hopes they fallow a drying world.

And I go on, listening to it all, hopeless

to it all. And apart from it. I have been abandoned.

And on every building I pass by

                    I am falling,

and as I walk along the river

                    I am drowning,

and every car that races me by

                    I am crumpling,

and in every plane I'm boarding

                    I'm descending.

What makes you so invulnerable? What makes you so special?

"The whole of time, if you look at it in this way, can be regarded

49

as no more than one single night." Christ: "The day

of the Lord will come as a thief in the night; in the which

the heavens shall pass away with a great noise, and the elements

shall melt with fervent heat, the earth also and the works

that are therein shall be burned up." We are always dying.

We are living just to die. We are always putting dead things

in our mouths – and who is putting us in theirs? And

this moment, neither good nor bad, is leaving and won't be remembered.

I used to think differently in my money-making days.

I thought, if I could stack coins up to heaven, if

I can keep pushing this shopping cart down the aisle, if I

can just keep paying rent, my time on this earth will be justified,

ever worthwhile. I thought opening up my wallet made me regular.

Now I just sit here

         observing the drops of light

                  wishing they were rain.

When you stop getting a paycheck,

                 you think your life has stopped.

Every dollar is a girlfriend, a car, a house, two children,

retirement, or even so soon as a restaurant, an opera,

a CD, a vacation, another bookcase. Your life stops,

the world closes to you, and you long for the paycheck again,

even reduced to beggary. Because your salary

is your worth. It's your passport. It's your

way around the world. And you're proud of that.

But you deny that your photo is on the passport.

That's my father's outlook on things. I know what he's

doing today too. He's going to supermarkets and warehouses

and hardware stores to see what their deals are, hauls them

into the car, pulls them into the basement, and at midnight

scrolls through pages of other deals on other days.

I don't know what else he could be doing. Maybe he keeps

a woman. Women are most receptive to money.

And money is so much of what he is,

even when he has never had a lot. It's the ideal,

more than anything, that something is coming in,

meaning something less to worry about. As money

buys everything. It buys cat food, it buys living

space, it buys doctor's appointments, and a walker

for grandma, it buys gas, it pays away debt,

it serves taxes, it forces maintenance, it fetches

tombstones, and it encourages the wife to be grateful.

But it can never

                    cure boredom, or make

one's children love you, or purchase respect,

or self-actualization, or reconciliation with one's

maker, or deter your wife, who "roasts her man

without a fire

                    and serves him up to a raw old age,"

neither will it resolve your daddy issues, so you won't

pass them down to your son. It pays for everything

else, so you can continue being a cog in the machine.

I don't blame him. I really don't. I would too,

if I were made normally. "You know, the gods
never let on

how humans might make a living."
If they did, we wouldn't be in such horrible need,
neither our needs be horrible too. All evil arrives
all at once. I can bend your ear about it, I could,
about the history of my people, the people who made need
a kind of god, the history of the Chinese people,

who have seen and suffered all sorts of cycles of fortune,
some emperors good, most dynasties bad, but we all stay the same,
growing rice on paddies, on the merciless ground, being frugal
with the few grains that come up fine, because whatever pecks
weren't taken by bandits or warlords calling themselves king
were god-given by a river that didn't overflow or an illness
that didn't overkill or the clouds that refused to rain sweet
holy water, and there are always mouths to feed, too many.

That's why we worship education. Someone in their fool head
had it in their mind to call "loyalty to me" as "wisdom",
and rewarded men for being smart when in reality they were being
obedient. This is why the Chinese nowadays hate Confucius,
for he reasoned that "if the ruler be not a ruler, the subject
not a subject, the father not a father, the son not a son,
then even if there be grain, would I get to eat it?"
If the world were as polite as Moore's paper nautilus, sure.

There are so many men who think the world can be ordered.
This is only good for he who wants or needs an ordered
world, and you bet he has a lot of money to make it happen

52

and protect himself when it doesn't. But for all the others,

they have no mouthfuls, though they're content with the scraps

of the man who does. Exams only elevate the few

to fool the many into thinking it's a good man generous

with grains, and not bad. But the Chinese believe it all the same,

as their bellies are empty, and the fight has long been snuffed out.

So we have worked ourselves to death – on the fields,

clutching withered roots, hanging our heads down low come home

with nothing for our children to eat, or in the palaces,

implementing orders, hoping that come the next emperor

we won't lose our heads or our dignity for disagreeing –

and we have admitted we are on the way of all death.

And that's how you have peace, when no one wants change.

And now we live in modern ways

                              wherein we are more crooked.

A lot of men think you can buy open the gates of heaven. A lot

think they are kings themselves – who hasn't wanted the dragon's robes? –

because their lucre buys them hands

                              that make their watches,

put wheels on their cars, massage them, send faxes

for them, prepare their meals, and educate their children

in computer and piano, a bunch of tools that

won't stop them from being sales associates or dishwashers,

or worse, sad, or slaves. Because what furnishes their wallets

Is servitude. It's giving up the right to say no. There's no getting round

being Chinese. No one likes us or has us around for our wit.

We're sellouts. There's no coin that can pay off our spiritual mortgage, the debt that accumulates from being ignorant and mean. Our fault

for living a life where a man in pajamas is a kind of god.

And this comes into relief when we speak

of the Pandemic.

What, were we not supposed to be called bat-munchers on Xi's behest?

No, I never really was comfortable being Chinese.

Chinatown to me was humid heat, dead fish in ice

pens, and men crouching over dirty stairwells, smoking

over their dirty aprons, tired. Even in America

being Chinese was akin to being a slave, caged

in the tenements other immigrants had passed down,

beneath polluted skies, being unable to fully

breathe free and plume beyond yourself.

That's pretty much why I only felt comfortable when

I was making money, as then I had a pass

and was allowed to weave my way around a world

that really didn't want me around, without green.

And yet I was still lost in the world, for I spoke

only in dollars. And yet, without dollars,

I fear all there is to me is silence. Men with money

aren't hollow, we were simply born that way.

And during the time of death and disease I

worked.

Because I got my paycheck, my life continued normally.

I still had my passport to live, while many lost theirs,

so I ignored them and continued on with my life

of carting groceries,

cooking stews, sleeping long on Sundays, with The Office on.
And I paid for it later. The universe balances itself out.
I don't believe in karma, but there's an end to profiting off
other's people's misery. For most, it comes later than it should.

And the rich men will one day hitch onto their rockets,
stuffing champagne and charcuterie into their pockets.
They fly higher and higher, knowing punishment is not in this life,
but their descendants and those after, they see justice as a knife.

Wealth is something suffered through. You have it,
everyone else doesn't. Nothing so inspires men to envy.
You find friends only in other rich men, who conspire
less to steal your bag, but you find the worth
of these friends lie largely in their riches, and riches
don't talk or take care of you when you're sick.
Your dollars are your only friends, and you rely on them
and not trust.
                And yet everyone prefers dollars.

But me nowadays, I just
                        strum. I'm not so wise
to abstain from money, but I've laid up enough
in store so as not to stress about it, for now.
But it baffles me that my diploma is a piece of paper.
It confuses me that, after years of working,
there is no more need for hands. The sun shines,
the birds sing, the earth continues its orbit around
the sun, and yet the world no longer needs any work.

I spend too many hours of the day suspecting

the hours we put into our work that others praise

as virtuous and necessary to the pillars of society

are indeed but smoke meant to keep us busy

and distracted from the hard ways of living and

consequently from expending energy against society,

a transaction not necessarily created from malice

but from the incompetence of the so-called leaders

of business whose minds can't comprehend their operations

and only the number of zeroes some dollar amounts contain

or the stuff they can shove into their office and point

to these that they are masters of realms as populated as Earth.

Sometimes I contemplate on the whole lot of stuff in the world

and how it comes from one sea and leaves distantly to another

and I do sometimes wonder if it all happens as a coincidence

and we have lost control of the machine or the machine is controlled

by the quiet and humble few who know the true destinations of stuff A

and stuff B, and they move like dung beetles, as in, slowly,

and then there are their managers who think they know but don't

and then there are the CEOs who make money from those who do.

I become more and more certain of this thought

when on the event of a plane crash or a tankard spill

somehow everyone goes unblamed except

for those who are silently fired, the rest, salaries slashed.

But, again, I don't think too much on it. Nowadays I just strum.

But a man needs to prove his worth. No man

wants their plowshare to grow dull.
When a man has too much time on his hands,
he permits too much space into his eyes,
the horizon he consumes from the windowsill
makes him dreamy, and thoughtless, then selfish,
he lets his good traits rust, he lays his virtues
in dust, until he's no good to the world.

Men need to work. A man should know he's needed
and that he most needs himself. When a man is
in his lonesome, who is his companion? When a man
doesn't defend himself, who is his attendant? Himself.
So he grows to distrust himself. As I am beginning
to. It's a shame crooked men know this too,
hoard all the work and give them to bad men,
make beggars of good ones by buying their goodwill.

There's no way around it. It seems money finds its way
into the hands of everyone but those who grow food
and guard their neighbors' stock. Every fool man
wants to find their gold mine and do no more work,
except to tell another man what to do. And they obey,
so long as their purses are full. These men could care
less about hardworking and saving dear in hard times,
they spend their days pilfering another man's pocket,

for they live in a dream where gold grows on trees.
I can't blame them. It's easy thinking in a world where
it seems someone will furnish your next meal. But who
gave it him? And who before? And who before?

It's no wonder people feel they owe nothing and yet are owed,

it's no wonder people feel they owe nothing to the earth

that gave birth to them, bunch of ungrateful sons,

and it's no wonder a man holds himself in high esteem, others low.

When men become robbers, and rob the poor blind

the ones after them rob, and the ones after them,

until from root to leaf the whole tree is rotten.

"Men were not born wolves, and they have become wolves."

And that was Confucius's real meaning: when no one cares a fig

for another and their own dignity, forget about eating.

A man would rather take than share during bad times,

even though blessings come from sharing. So his time was called

the Warring States. "Bellum omnium contra omnes."

And all this plays out in how men

                    value art,

a kind of contraption that grows no wheat and

makes no milk to drink, but feeds a man's spirit

in a world that inspires only dread.

                    If no art

were in this world, I wouldn't want to live in it,

would happily give it all away, awaiting

the next or the void of all souls. "Whosoever drinketh

of the water that I shall give him shall never thirst."

Art is the window which

                    the soul shows through.

On dark days I

went me to the museum,
and observed Rothko's roving fields, Monet's molten
earth, Millet's pious farmers, Rodin's marble oceans,
van Gogh's blazing wheat, the stations of the Cross,
mandalas, portraits of Americans, Dutch flowers,
Menkaura, boats of the dead, Roman busts,
snuff boxes, calligraphy, and Chinese saucers,

and I would lay my voice so quiet, I would hear
the floorboards creak under me and the ventilation
overhead, and I would swish side to side, observing
from one angle to another, moving backward and
forward, letting the thing become big in my view,
or focusing on one place over the other, then
making it small, or seeing the thing entire,
because, to me, art is a field of color and space,

color and space which we communicate with,
color and space that we argue with, that we
question the world as we see it, and present the world
that the artist is arguing, and then these worlds mixing
comes out a world broader and more colorful.
Thus art is our means of speaking to the dead,
we hold a conversation in blues and reds
and daubs and tempura, and we feel a little less

in our loneliness. Because artists create for
Stendhal's "happy few". These men and women
have seen all manners of cruelties and sufferings,
passions and follies and joys, finding them

inexpressible but in the vertigo of color
and in the brushstroke like the wind raking the sand
or water coursing through mud; in short, the brush
is an interruption in life, as powerful as God's

own hand which guides with a strong mind the tracks
of our days without relying on sheer force. When I
did not value my own life, I went to the museum
and taught myself their music, and felt if they
earned some mastery over their lives in spite of
the overwhelming misery of their lives, then there may
be some hope for me. And their mastery is this: in the frame
is beauty only, and thus in the frames of our soul is beauty only.

Only the meagerest men think

      Monet's view of the Epte
has a price, or that van Gogh's sunflowers

       need admission,
or depictions of the Pietà, an evaluation, or Pollack's saxophone
squiggles, or Basquiat's Six Crimee, need an auction,
as then their value will appreciate. We're not appreciative.
These artists are raped. Their hands are covered by our hands.
We neuter them on marble tiling. We plaster over
their messages. We make commission off of their souls.

When we look at paintings, we admire

      their price at Sotheby's.
Then these works lay in storage, because they're too dear
to look at. Tell me, if art is the window into the artist's soul,
then what shall we call the voyeur? A crank! A masturbator!

Someone who doesn't see the subject, but their orgasm!
A pervert! with only one aim:

> to see how far he can debase himself.

And writers have it no better. We think because writing
is words, there's something more direct, less obscure,
more noble about it. But that's not true. Of the writers
to make it out alright, well, Faulkner by fifty found fame.
Eliot, the Nobel. But everyone else is Dante or Melville
or Joyce, or Whitman, or Dickinson. They sing songs
not for everyone, but for you. They sing songs to remind
you, after so many abuses, of your humanity. But

no one will pay for that. Humanity is not a quantity.
It's not measured in ounces or pounds, nor in meters
or voltage; it goes unmeasured in our souls until
it is compared to our misery and poverty. And adversity
is something people with dollars do not like.
They attempt to buy all adversity away. Some of them
accomplish just that, and so their ability to feel
dries up with your buyout. There's nothing noble about the Nobel.

Perhaps this just means

> art has no value

in this or the next world. If God so loved artists
he could give them peace of mind, or a place
to rest their souls on. But James feared unimportance,
Whitman went ignored, Hölderlin went mad,
and Gertrude was considered depressed. (She probably was.)
And if God does not reward their work, because

he does not want anyone praising his world,

then there must be very little beauty in his world.
And so if man finds beauty in the artist's works,
this must be a misinterpretation. Meaning is a
mirror; in our descriptions are our biases.
In James we can find a kind of modern masculinity
or a denunciation of man as a concept, in exchange
for something more universal. I mean, who gives a shit?
And in finding our own meaning in their objects,

these objects which are their last memories of
their mothers, their homes, their histories,
their sadnesses, their moments of triumphs,
we ransack and pillage them of their humanity, finally.

And the things in their lives dying,
they die their second death. And when finally
forgotten, they die their third death,
and then their fourth when they're slandered.

Because, you know, James was a Dead White Man.

But that's okay, for a lot of people believe
they don't die in their bodies, they die at home.

And as for me, well, why do you think I sing this song?
I must be a fool for going on singing. Well, you're right,
I am a fool. Plato told Ion

                that art is a kind of magic

fooling its listener into believing it is real, or art

is an address from the gods through which the singer

is merely their sower of choice for their wisdom.

So, yes, I am a fool: I feel if I stop singing,

I suddenly stop believing in goodness in this world.

Life is me just yelling

                         into the wind. It's selfish, I know.

But what else am I to do? If I stop, then I know

I no longer believe that our hearts can be reached,

that we can communicate the great and the good, and aim

for them, and if I no longer believe, what hope is there left

for something as small as me? If I stop singing, I die.

It's a pity all I can do is sermonize. I'm a blunt instrument.

A kind of stupid, boorish god is animated through me.

In the basement I see statues

of Guanyin, cans of cranberry

sauce, seltzer, old newspapers,

but nothing anymore of my father.

He has covered himself up.

He has given himself away.

A tax to Mammon.

And I'm killing myself slowly

by killing him gradually

in the darkness of my mind.

When I was bullied, he never stood up for me.

When I was confused, he was never concerned.

When I was mistaken, he blamed me.

When I was lost, he said, just follow me,

and do as I tell you.

                    I resented him.

Well what was he supposed to do?

                              And yet I

resented him. I disbelieved him all my life.

And yet I said nothing. And I followed him.

And to my bullies too I said nothing.

And when they insulted me, I said nothing.

And when I lost my job, I said nothing.

And when I wanted to kill myself, I said nothing.

And I sat so many times saying nothing in the passenger's seat

hearing him hate his wife, my mother,

                              curse her

for her meanness, lack of consideration, her greed,

thought I was the proper audience, for he already threw himself away.

The same pained thoughts whose circle sleep

doesn't and possibly never shall cease.

A blue morning succeeds a sleepless night.

I'm emptying an apartment, leaving some

six years of memories, throwing some of it away.

Parents arguing. Ever too many things to do.

Father driving too fast – angry over some

self-imposed deadline i.e. over nothing.

Eruption in left ear. I want to say something. I don't.

Car swerves left. We hit the Jersey wall, though

we're not in New Jersey. I see myself and my parents dying.

Airbag blows up, like a ghost or archangel. Darkness.

Looking back, never once thinking we would be ten o' clock news.

Pelted by glass. Mother screams. I imagine

her flying through the windshield.

Some silence. A kind of limbo. Begged to come out.

Every person and every question is less irritating,

not irritating at all, even a bit beautiful however beyond.

People stop and go. I call them the salt of the earth.

Elbow, finger, head. Mother sad her clavicle is blood colored.

Tire is on fire. Car is not. It spun a

full one-eighty, spilling fuel the while.

Father wants his wallet. I call him

psychotic. Wonders why I'm crying.

Why did we not die? Why am I alive? Not sure if asking

means I don't want to live or I ought to be or

I owe someone for it. That fuel was like my future,

there was more of it than I would have surmised.

When the lights went out, I did not think, I want to live,

I thought, this must be it. I must be a murderer.

Mother swears car was near tipping over.

No, I don't want to talk. Let them harp.

Everyone in texts is sympathetic. I

do not sympathize with everyone.

Finding pieces of broken glass and black

fuzzy specks in my hair all day.

I same as see with second sight, seared into my iris

or skull, the darkness, our bodies crushed like bugs,

the exact sequence, play by play. I don't

even remember prom or my birthday.

My father is a big wide word, unresolved. Forgive

and forget, or fingerpoint. I'm not pointing fingers,

nor am I forgiving. There is but this doubt,

that must cloud over us from now on.

Today's Wordle is "Guile."

Unsure what it all means. Need to know

if it has meaning. In the night train, alternating

between sobbing silently and staring at the ceiling.

Closing my eyes is time traveling back to

that blue morning succeeding a sleepless night.

I almost died. But all I think about is:

You were willing to throw your life away.

You didn't try to protect yourself nor did you

shy away from the thought, as befits humility.

You were willing to throw your life away because

you hate it. You only have one life, dude.

And yet I still hate my life. I would still give it away.

Our soul is a clouded dish, or a pretty flower,

that a better angel holds in their palms and says

Please take care of this, this is all of your life.

And yet we drop it. It falls so effortlessly.

I try to love my father. I don't want him to go

away. I want to be close to him. I want

to help him, I want to make sure he isn't hungry

when he comes home late at night. But there's

nothing for us to share. We're two empty things

because we have scooped out our souls and thrown

them away. And sometimes I do indeed blame him for that.

What good is a father if his son doesn't hold onto his heart?

Sometimes I want to say, Why can't you be my father for once?

Fighting is a family's favorite pasttime. Family is being born
among people who resemble and lay some claim on you.
"Familiarity breeds contempt." You learn to hate
from your family, sometimes by hating them, sometimes by watching
them, sometimes by their taking what is yours – food,
favor, fate. There are no happy families in the Bible,
siblings fight each other as they fight God. "Happy families
are all alike; every unhappy family is unhappy in its own way."

We try to find family among friends and acquaintances.
That's a laugh. How are you companionable when you hate yourself?

I'm fighting beneath the lamppost wrapped in diamond dust.
I'm fighting in a wicker chair beside my ice melting.
I'm fighting with my back turned as I clean the dishes.
I'm fighting while I keep my gaze on the dusty sidewalk,

and that same night I cried, and that same night I longed to apologize,
and when she did not accept it, I wanted to die. I held
myself on the street, I held myself on benches, I held
myself on the studio floor – I couldn't sleep anymore in bed –
and when I couldn't stand it, their footsteps over me, the police
sirens cutting me, from the window slats like knives,
I tried to apologize again, and I still was refused,
and that was when I wanted to die

                              and then I

wanted to make her my enemy, if she wouldn't be my friend.

I don't know why I did that. I don't know how it made sense to me.
I always thought myself considerate. I thought myself gentle.
I always thought myself harmless. I don't know how I got so mad.
But it defined me. It left a scar. It left a "callus
on my soul." My rage made me human.

                                        And beautiful.

I never knew who I really was until I hated someone.
Love has limits. Love has a price ceiling. We celebrate love
only once a year. The other three hundred and sixty four,
we reserve for hatred. And contempt.

                                I never admitted,

until then, I was a hating thing. Anger to me was a fault.
Wrath was sin. No. Wrath is being human. When
I was alone at night, I punched her desk. I tipped
her pencils over. I rubbed my ass on the place where she
worked. When I saw her, I gave her the cold shoulder; when
she extended the olive branch, I gave her my contempt;
and then, I would wish her happy birthday, or
praise her hard work, so that she would keep extending
that branch, just so I could slap it out of her hand.
And, I gritted my teeth and cursed her, at night. For.
Five. Years. Again, I don't know why I did it either.
It was not a coordinated or conscious effort. I just did
it, as if I were born with the ability to keep grudges.

When Cain slew Abel he knew he went against God's will,
and indeed before he held the knife in his hand
he felt he was all in accord with God; but by killing
Abel he became greater than God, he killed God,

and became his own master, even if only for a moment.
What does it matter what came after? He knew God
hated him before, hated him then, would hate him after.

And after those five years, I no longer felt anger.
I did not feel any loss, unlike other appetites.
Anger is an inferior exultation, but exultation all the same.

Revenge was telling my father I didn't trust him.
Revenge was telling my mother she was stupid.
Revenge was telling my friends they were wrong.
Revenge was telling women they were whores.
I liked the reactions they gave. It's because they
realized there was some truth in what I said.
Otherwise, there wouldn't have been a reason to be upset.
I enjoyed reminding them of what they were
as I'm reminded everyday of what I am.

When I hated her, I felt the world was alright.
I didn't feel any fear. How could I, when my body was light?
I feared no retaliation. It's not like there couldn't be.
Where fear prevented me from speaking out before, from
showing myself before, here it hid itself.
I felt the world was finally just, and it was filled with light,
like the truth had been obscured, and now it was made clear,
and I knew all my life I was set here to curse her.

Though, and it is true, sometimes I feared on the morrow
I would enter the office doors and find her desk empty
and in the corner lingering by the ferns and the window find

a coworker of mine crying, explaining to me she had died,
or I would be given a phone call from my mother and hear
that a train my father was on had careened; I feared much
the guilt stinking from my curses, as if God had punished me
by listening to me and answering my desire to become a god,

but practice confirms he doesn't bother listening to me
and so I proceed with my dawn full of wishful thinking.

Those were the days I believed in nothing.
No, nothing-believing is not negating.
Believing is not just believing in a god
who split heaven and earth and made the mind,
belief is believing your girlfriend loves you,
belief is believing your child will lead a better life,
belief is believing there is something decent in people,
belief is believing the things we do are not in vain.

The things we believe in that get our days going
are unfounded. Tomorrow is simply not today,
the bonds keeping us with our girl become bad,
the circumstances that allowed us our hoards decay,
the dignity in others are covered with indifference,
and the morality and justice we believe are sparks of light
to the next generation are courtesies holding them back.
What is bright to us is dark in others, what is good to one man

is another man's stumbling block, and men's sight is so unclear
that we would rather bicker than agree on what "bad" can be,
and in fact make our evils our gods, for what else do we know?

That's believing in nothing; it's not negating belief,

it's not a reluctance to believe, it's simply a refusal

to accept anything can be truthful, and to hold one's self fast

in the ever-raging winds of the present, rooting oneself

to the seemingly stable ground and denying the rain its reality.

I found this total darkness of the soul comforting.

Every morning I rode the train sleeping on my hands,

entered the elevator, ascended to the office,

and resumed work, hating my coworkers and the

headache mounting from sleepless nights unending,

and, the sun set down and the sky painted black, descended

the elevator as my soul did, took the train back home,

feeding another day to the complete meaningless of my life,

and meaninglessness, indeed, gathers meaning from daily living.

We feed it our biases, our wrong assumptions, our denials,

which daily betray us when our enemies point out our wrongs,

when we feel the shame that comes from bad living

and seeing in others our impotency, in spite of theirs.

Meaninglessness is a kind of god, one that protects us

from leaving this life too soon, by preventing us

from questioning our vapid existence and amending it.

But meaninglessness is only good for those who can afford it.

Come the blast of misfortune, there is no person who does not

scramble, hold as many possessions in their hands, and cry,

Dear Lord, why me? and shall we chastise them, saying,

You cry to no one, to no one do your things have meaning,

same as your life, in fact it is no different if you died than if you lived,

so you should rejoice, for you now see the real value of existence?
Who really permits themselves to live in Diogenes' barrel?

That we are alive

                    means we find meaning in living,
even if that meaning is that we prefer it than its opposite
for no reason than we're in the thick of it, and indeed Diogenes
at the end of the day still ate and slept, and did not do their opposites
though that would have been true freedom. Giving us meaning
was God's greatest curse. Our body is a shackle,
and yet we are afraid to break it. Why do we hope?
We know the limits of our vessel; why hold out for revelation?

Indifference and rudeness hardens in us from hard living
and forms a shell through which our words are muffled
and winged through, and words from armor are armored words,
and tell the receiver, treat me delicately and treat me kind
for I have wounded and been wounded in the past. And perceiving
nothing in the nightness of our armor, we find only silence
will stay as our companion. And so with silence we are familiar.
Silence should be a thrill, an invitation to learn
more about ourselves and our bodies, but we use the chance
to learn more why to hate and how to wound ourselves
and retreat and add more layers onto our armor.
These same men

                    harden their hearing when they see any words come,
for they know every word seeks them to stand aside their armor
and on every other wound them and remind them of the armor's sake.
And therein they sit, rewinding every memory of their pain.

We were not made "machine men, with machine minds and machine hearts."
But our reason

    is a machine, and most human in me is reason.
If we were born into the bodies of plants, perhaps we would not hate.
If we were born to a forgiving earth, there would be no reason for war.
But neither is true. We were born with bombing brains and striking
souls, and these weapons implanted into us are not meant for the evils
of hunger and thirst and neglect and fear, but against our brothers.
If you praise God, you must praise him for making us murderers.
I hate God. And hating God, it doesn't matter if I hate any other.

I really don't know why I did it. She's out of my life now.
I want to apologize to her.

    But I wouldn't change a thing.
Because the very act of living is a sin, it doesn't matter who
we punish with our hatred. Today it's her, tomorrow it's someone
else, and she has wounded people too. Ultimately it was just.
"Is there not rain enough in the sweet heavens
to wash it white as snow?" What does it matter
if we pile more filth onto this filthy world?

Fuck the world.
Fuck the world!
FUCK THE WORLD.

The city of Dis is big and wide enough,
but not a soul may breathe in it.
Smooth are its smooth walls running up
into blackest infinity, running up too
are its exhaust fumes, painting the sky dark.

O sky whose rain is blood, whose dirt

grows no roots, whose mouths are hungry

and feed only on beauty, and whose merchandise

is misery, and whose ceiling is twisted tinsel and steel,

how does any soul live in you and your walls

which are a cage whose bars are

illness and age and fear and rage?

"Yeah the doctors don't know

New York was killing me."

The angels hammered into demons

eye me warily from the battlements.

I come upon them like a celebrity.

What human willingly enters the blast of hell?

And yet I too make my residence in hell.

And yet I said, if we cannot be equals,

then know what it is to be my enemy.

If you're so omnipotent, why don't you stop me?

Bill, to live in outrage

                    is better than not living at all.

And I was never supposed to sing for so long,

but then again, I never knew how to sing songs.

Fancy that. Singing songs for most of my life,

and all of them bad ones.

There was always an arrogance in singing songs.

There was always an arrogance in supposing my voice

elevated above others. When I began writing,

I wanted some girl to love me. She's not important,

though I still love her now. And I suppose

my admitting this means there is folly in singing still.

When I sang, I was an ugly little,

mean little, little minded man, and I hoped

that the song would dress me as I wasn't.

I thought if I loved the song as much as I loved her,

then the song would reward me with its mysteries.

I made the Marriage of Figaro and Marcellus's Mass

my fears and my imperfections. I revered them,

these great songs, and I devoted my hours

to emulating their majesty and movement. But look

at me now, squawking and squealing, lamenting

about the loves I never had, and the loss that I am.

Music does not make a man of me. What a mistake

those hours spent were. Because music is a vanity too,

there's no meaning to music, though I thought there was.

I did not realize alliteration was vain, measure was vain,

rhyme was vain, and metaphor was vain, and in wanting to relate

in her vanity I was trying to impress her with mine.

I thought I could spin nothing into meaning, show her nothing

could blossom into love, but nothing is nothing,

is what floods our souls, is what fills our silence,

silence is all what poetry is.
                              Silence is the heart

of all music, because silence accompanies our doubt.

Silence is the language of an uncaring, unloving God.

Silence lasted in the womb, and silence stays in the void.

Silence and its consequent music made me realize I

could not love her nor anyone.

                              For a time I believed

if I asked piously at the altar of vanity, I would be blessed

as I always desired to be. But I lacked the sly skill

artists use to conceal the faults of life. I can't paint

scenes, I can't muster images, I don't do well with drama,

I find tragedy trite, I find the lovesick laughable,

I'm too clever to be witty, and to me the twist is tiring.

I have no ability to captivate an audience. I write

ugly poor songs. Perhaps that is who God is: a poor artist

like me, and all his creations are aborted songs.

There is nothing dazzling or exciting about me.

And when I move my mind to meaning, I find every reason

to be horrified, such that I think, who can write on this?

Writers never write, therefore, about what is real;

how many stale nights can be put on the page?

or, how many photos of corpse-strewn valleys

actually flood the soul into sympathy, and then action?

If art is so complete in convincing humans of humanity,

then why do we not live and refrain from making a compassionate world?

Is it because words are inadequate? Or are strings insensitive?

Why can I not express to my fellow the perils facing him and I?

If language is unable, then let us, please, head to the forge

and fashion a purer, more noble one. No, the issue

lies not with language, it lies with man's heart.

When we say "kindness", we dilute it until we're considered pure.

When we say "wisdom", we adulterate it until we're rich with it.

When we say "justice", we shorten it until we're tall.

Words are shining things, dew dropped from the heavens upon our dark path,

to lighten our way through the valleys of this earth, and yet

when we don't measure to them we become proud and debase them.

And that's what art is: a debasement of meaning.

I was a fool for looking for pure concepts in an impure implement.

I hate art, I insult art, I renounce art,

is what I want to say, if I did not now believe,

in the hour of my need, that I need to fool myself again

to have just one respite in this dark world, Eurydice.

I have composed a song not pretty, not abloom

with the joys and pleasures of the world above and over.

I sing a song of ugliness, the only song I can sing –

I am a small vessel, Lord, forgive me for falling short –

I sing a song disguising nothing, concealing nothing,

no blush on a girl's face, no brightness of youth,

I sing a song plain and straight about the things of this earth

as I see them plain and straight, and I play it

not to swoon your hearts, nor to soothe your senses

as songs ingeniously and insincerely do, I sing

so you know and know only how I feel –

and if you find the subject of my song small,

then you must conclude the world is small;

and if you find the subject of my song is rude,

then you must conclude the world is rude;

and if you find the subject of my song is dim,

then you must conclude the world is dim,

and that I am all of these things too.

And so now you listen, demons, shades, fallen angels all,

I don't fear you, and I don't look down at you,

because you have heard my words, you have a heart for hearing,

and that means you are human, despite your cruelties and follies.

I sing for you, you flinthearted fiends, I sing

so you may let me descend into the scream

77

                                              of existence;

don't mistrust me, and fear no punishment on my account,

I go willingly

                    because I no longer love life

                                              and I

am desperate to love after loving so little and so late.

I would plunge into these loveless realms. You who have never

been loved, who have always been reminded of your ugliness,

how can you find it in your hearts, however distorted, to deny me?

Bill, do you hear

                    the sound of arms clashing? Those are

the din of the horns of demons locking as they relate

to the other in bloodthirsty conflict. They fill the air

with gruntings, moanings, and roars, and

the earth of Dis is dead, watered by their sweat and blood

whereas ours replies to our labors with roots.

Bill, that shrieking in the distance is the lightning

of the lances the nephilim wield, when they throw them

from the heights of Dis down into the valleys below

where they piece through the flesh of some unfortunate.

Bill, you set to sea against the Third Reich,

you saw the ribs of those encamped in Auschwitz,

you saw smoke rise from the tankers of the Suez,

you saw helicopters flee en masse from Saigon,

and you feared, daily, that from your window a flash

of white light would obliterate all you loved and held dear,

but I see by your sidelong glance that you're still not numb

to violence. Bill, I must become insensate to these sights

                              78

if I hope to see the king of the dead, but you shouldn't

have to lose your humanity on my behalf. And yet

if you can accompany me, I may arrive whole.

Bill, you're an arse, but what I'm saying is: please, abide by me

as we descend into the rage of the world,

greater than the rages of our mediocre days,

a rage so extraordinary and extreme

so as to seem pure and for its own sake

it seems we are plunging into God's brains,

sniff out his designs for the universe

and find out precisely how we are damned.

For doesn't it seem,

                indeed, it's so common so as not to be blasphemous,

God loves to kill Jews? loves to kill Arabs? loves to smash Serbs

and the Tutsi into bits? thinks garroting blacks is funny,

thinks nailing nuns hilarious, and sees something sentimental

in raping Nigerian girls who haven't seen the firsts of womanhood?

same as priests sodomizing choir boys before their voices come in?

and if not, why are they, under his supposedly patient gaze?

Bill...why?

If we

are made

in God's image,

why

do we maim and

fuck God's creations?

Why do we

feel excruciating need

to tear out the eyes

and saw off the limbs

and drill the hymen

of someone's daughter,

some stranger we hadn't known

and can't, and won't, sympathize with

and somehow treat our neighbors

with more civility?

It's almost as if

civility and violence

are partners

and cooperate with the other

to form the resultant human

and his virtue and his wisdom.

This contradiction

is in every man

and it is in God too.

Is this how we reconcile Christ to the Old Testament?

the Old Testament telling of a deity who raised Israel,

then slandered them,

                then punished them,

                                hated them,

revenged himself on them,

                        all for his own insecurity

and the perceived slights against him?

                              Did Jesus

come out like a bitch,

                          apologized to those neck beards,

so that the Jews wouldn't pursue other deities?

Is this what the world is, a cosmic scam,

some asshole's voyeuristic interest in our suffering,

someone jacking off while we raise our voices in pain,

the crescendo, the revelation of our despair, the climax?

And did God inspire the Romans to crucify his son

when he was near giving the whole artifice away?

Is God a nut, is he neurotic, is he anxious, or depressed,

is he a screw-up, is he flaccid, did he say, It seemed like

a good idea at the time, and then just left,

and we deal primarily with his absence, and in truth,

there is nothing divine in our thought – no,

there is nothing divine in our destiny, and we are no more

than clockwork ticking toward infinity, and the measure of the machine

is the body count of our ingenious weaponry and administration?

When a man scouts for his prey,

some young thing wandering innocently,

and he searches through their features

for something specifically he seeks,

what runs in his head? does his mind

go through the memories of his past, and make

him at the moment the master of a trauma

where he had been helpless and alone, as this

innocent person is? does this conquest fulfill

some appetite slumbering in him, something

transferred over from our days as hunters,

and he felt complete in a world that permits him

the hunt, the action forgiving him the hunt,

and his body serving him in the hunt: or does he

look upon this creature, "this citadel of virtue,

wisdom, power," and see in them a kind of killing

of himself, that self that failed him once, and a killing

of God, who failed him all life and ever after,

and in so killing, finally making the world just

by killing someone they know is so throughly a dirtbag?

What does the act of killing entail? Do we see something of a human

in that which we plunge our blades into? or rather, must we turn them,

as by the magic called rhetoric, into objects and we are stabbing

but sacks of flour? but isn't God too an object,

for in his mind he filled the void of the universe with a rain

of things, and so isn't God also spatial and colorful

and material, and so when the commandant aims

through the scope of his gun the boy whose brown pupil

he sees plain and vibrant on the white sclera and holds weakly

the trigger that will burst and kick back, with a shake

of gunpowder, and make a bloody star of the boy, does that warrior

see something godlike in the boy too, namely the edict

that the universe was made for our play, and these boys,

jumping over the fences and running to the outskirts of camps, as toys?

There is something artistic in hurting. We express

our longtime hatred of the world in damaging,

in inflicting pain. We raise our bloody fists and roar,

yes, yesterday I was a lamb, but today I am a champion,

and this body, supposedly holy, is proof of that!

or does hurting interrupt some thought of ours

that we will be punished for our transgressions, and seeing

the smoking gun in our hand, the hole in the head,

and nothing but the darkness as witness to the act,

do we feel the earth becomes freer, the earth becomes more pure,

we know the earth now, it is not fragile to our bloody minds,

it is in fact receptive, she in fact removes her dress,

opens up her cunt, and tells us lustily to plunge away?

Does killing make us a kind of god? Does killing

implicitly kill the god who made us feel guilt, made us feel

shame, doubted us, stepped on us, begrudged us every bite,

or does killing demonstrate there are no gods except

the all-powerful god of death who answers our prayers

by removing everyone who expressed disappointment with us,

and this pleases us because our opinions are all we are,

and this pleases us because we already have so much cause to doubt

ourselves, and this removal makes us powerful by lack of counterpoint?

Is death a kind of god who creates absences

and the absence of pain, the absence of ambition?

Does death answer our innermost wishes,

as Freud described residing in the wills of boys:

that the world would be just upon ridding

ourselves of our fathers, our mothers-in-laws,

snake oil salesmen, politicians and Mormons?

Oh the joys I felt on contemplating

the smile on my face imagining

the day I would kick open the office door

imparting final gifts to my coworkers of

83

the rattling of the submachine gun

every brain blooming like anemones

the blood slopping in pools on the carpet,

their hands raised to defend themselves or

beg for mercy which I answer with

a kick from my jack-knife boots,

cutting their exposed bellies with a bullet

spilling their guts like ribbons out of the slit

or the thrall accompanying

the stroll to the halls of

Congress where their withering and whitened heads turn

to see me grinning ear to ear as I raise the grenades

high over my head and watch them fall down like

hail in January or rain deep into calendar May,

and though Shakespeare said mercy "droppeth as the gentle rain

from heaven upon the place beneath" these

tokens of my mirth burst into plumes of smoke,

obscuring the desks and lecterns but a while,

to then lift and clear and reveal the pattern

of their lacerated forms on the antique carpet,

the bodies of those who felt leading the hopeless

was a lesser pursuit compared to lining their pockets

with touring ghostwritten books and insider trading.

And in Charlottesville what went through the driver's mind

as he hit the gas into the throng of people, those protestors

whom he thought thought little of him, well now he would show them

he thrilled to the thought of their hips smashing into the hood,

their bodies denting the bumper, and the audible snapping

of their spines, leaping into his ears like the

84

ascension of Brunhilde's voice in the Götterdämmerung?

Or Sandy Hook, with his twenty-two caliber rifle,

what went through his mind as he watched those

little bodies, full of potential, which was denied him,

crumpled before him? Did he think, this is fish in the barrel,

or, watch their little legs scurry, or, why

won't they defend themselves? or did nothing

occur in his heart, did he feel then

the rifle in his hand, his mission in his mind,

he was complete and fulfilled in the universe?

Did these men feel the strains of patriotism throb

within their hearts when they heard how

the American troops stormed the beaches of Normandy

and gave their lives to defeat a vast evil,

and, dying with a warrior's weapon in hand, accomplished

the purpose of their birth, finding their place on Earth?

And these same men were directed to place their hand on their heart

and sing songs on how noble it is to sacrifice a life.

"Hector, you madman, don't stand there babbling to me of covenants,

there are no faithful oaths between lions and men,

nor do wolves and lambs have any oneness of heart,

but they are always at fatal odds with each other."

This is how the Athenians convinced their young men

to fight with bravery and manliness in their battles, by

goading them from shrinking into their shields, and withholding

their spears, in the fear that when they returned to the polis

they would face humiliation enough that they would like to die.

And this is how, starving and diseased, the Athenians
ended a charming campaign in the Peloponnese.

And in the Aeneid, "Five full circles they run and
reel and as many back, around and back,
for it's no mean trophy they're sporting after now,
they race for the life and lifeblood of Turnus."
In the dead man's eyes do we recognize something like
regret? Do we think there is still defiance in him
lasting him after the battle, or does it suffice
he sees the shadow of the blade raised over his head,
no childhood toys here, and in one brilliant flash,
a decisive cut blessed by the noonish sun, his life
is severed from his body, and his soul ranges down
the darkened rivers leading into the lands of the dead?
Is Turnus, impetuous man, so completely unqualified
for mercy? But it's too late – Turnus, who has
died a thousand deaths since Aeneas, standing tall
and triumphant, laid him long on the ground, is now
cut in twain, and is out of the reaches of hope.

And isn't Bond the modern-day counterpart,
pointing his gun at Goldfinger, the modern
stand-in for Turnus, a foreign actor
whose hoards are not his own but the property
of the people, as in, Bond's people? Don't the Avengers
kill a lot of differently-skinned aliens? And then there's
Batman, who revenges on the straw people of our fears.

No, I don't want to be Batman. Who wants

to be Batman? It appears a lot of men
want to be Batman, want to get the girls
like Batman, want to be a billionaire like
Batman, want washboard abs just like
Batman's, and want to be authoritative on all
things good and just like Batman.
But the reel ends, the projector lights
dim, and on the silver screen it's evident
Batman isn't real. But the illusion is set:
the men say, I want to be Batman,
I shall live in a world of only villains but one hero,
I shall live in a world where death accompanies justice,
I shall live in a world where beauty flows through
so long as I beat up those who defer,
and isn't Batman a convenient vehicle to criticize
all those who prefer deliberation over decisiveness?

And I think, oftener than those aforementioned, on
he who, on New Year's Day, saw so little worth
in his body so as to put it inside a truck
stacked tall with explosives, and awaited the frightening
and howling moment when his body would be burst
and burnt in flames and thundering. Did he think
pain would accompany, or would there be oblivion alone
before he approached a maker who would call him man enough?
Is this what masculinity is – that of the male body
being dieted and drilled, and driven long lengths
across the world to fire at distant targets obscured
in the dust of the desert in the name of defense;
is this a man's purpose, to give away his life

to some fool president on the debt that he won't be forgotten,

and on returning home, his body deformed into a weapon,

he finds his home unrecognizable, himself unneeded,

and as ultimate penance for giving his life as a surety

to another he makes good on his mistakes by ending it,

because he didn't have the honesty to say, even I need love too?

And then we weep, oh how we weep, weep ourselves so violent

a storm over these poor fellows' graves, and say with our pastors

that their souls art in heaven, yes, with seventy-two virgins,

yes, a heaven luminous and white and not stained with blood

yet a heaven peculiarly open to those dyed in blood,

and those who remain on earth, who have their lives still,

to whom we should yell, for God's sake, hold onto this life.

They think, hands on their rifles, oh heaven, sweet heaven,

heaven of inexpressible bliss I shall go

                           when I accept

the bullet destined for me and with my name on it?

Life is

      justice for me, no mercy for you.

Some slit-eyed, laughing governor thinks

a life should be given unto ideals, like

Andromeda given unto the sea serpent, while he,

on a cold day, warms in the armchair of his manor.

What does it matter? Who cares if you die?

I am alive – isn't that an accomplishment?

Yes, in a world where it is hard to live, I

am alive, and you aren't, and that seems

to point to God's design. If you are dead,

well, God bless your soul, I know I'm

doing right by him.

And so Emmet

died with eyes wide open, and he floated

down the river, unrecognizable to his mother,

unrecognizable to the men who put him there,

who had the greater burden to ensure

he held onto the form he entered the earth

as God intended he should and was right to keep.

And what did they think? Perhaps they thought,

if my skin were dark too, I would let me

do the things I did to him, as they tied

barbed wire around his neck, to weigh his body down

watching it

descend

into the waters below,

as they figured all life must eventually go.

What shall we tell Emmet, in here halls of the dead?

that it's not a matter of skin color, or the way he talked,

or his behavior, or his method of ambulating, rather

it's a man asking, God, how can you have a man

drink my water, breathe my air, and ravish my women

and I have none myself? and in his impotency he raises

his revolver and aims it square in the face of God, and says,

if I survive, I have earned my right to live.

And in that moment, it was true.

But everyone

eventually dies. And who doesn't

                              bear the scars
of the moment, when they tried to defy God?
He is always holding

                    the revolver in his hand and
pointing it at the boy just fourteen years of age
and he is always intending to kill him, one bullet down
the brain, and extinguish the flickers of life in him,
and he is always holding the revolver

                              on the field,
in the store, in the dark of night in his bed, and he is always
listening to the bullet fly fast in the air, fly so quickly
sometimes he thinks it flies into his own skull and comes out
the other end and in the silence of the aftermath he sees
only darkness and, a premonition from God, the faint glow
of fire in that darkness, so that he wakes up and sweats
the bed, goes to the mirror, examining himself but lightly,
and asks, there is no money in the till, there are aches
up my spine, and my head is going blind,
so, my God, why do you insist on cursing me?
And to this question there is no answer, and he suspects
he deserves no answer, for he did not precede with,
what have I done wrong?

We run round and round, and round and round,
and in so doing isn't that God's intending,
that we keep running in circles of
killing our enemies today, so they muster the vigor
into killing us tomorrow, and so on and so forth
unto the end of eternity, or, so we fear, unto neverending,
that the universe is not made of goodness and beauty

                              90

but blood and body and tears and life is always

succeeded by death, meaning someday

the future dies too, that this then means there is

no future, and we are holding in our sweaty hands

the grenade, the AR-15, the nuclear launch codes,

because we are most ourselves in genocide,

we are most human in massacre,

we are beautiful in our obligation to destroy,

most profound in seeing the rolling hills and the

endless green of the earth as distances

for the tanks to tread over and wood to cut

for the stock of our carbines or abodes of the natives

for our napalm to set ablaze? Weren't we splendid

in painting the Viet Cong as numbers,

and all we had to do was lower the number by ones and tens

until the war was over? How much in one missile?

Some thirty million dollars to kill thirty some chinks?

Then the solution to the war is elementary school math.

In war there is no valor, only material,

the men who fill the barracks are but ammunition

no different than the charge or the cannonball

designed to be put into certain slots and deployed

into certain theaters and die the right deaths

at the right place at the right time with the right attitude.

Man is most profound when forsaking his humanity.

There is never a day when a dog is not a dog,

a doe not a doe and a gull pretends it's anything other,

and yet we became master of all animals when we

deny ourselves emotion and forsake our lives

by seeing ourselves as but the number one.

91

But doesn't the dog possess even the common sense
to defend himself with the knowledge he will die?

And after causing the killing of everyone
and the culling of those who see us in differing eyes,
when we look round, who will be left? only those
who have blood painting their hands; and so blood
shall be the paint of one's eternal kingdom on earth,
and kingdom so created, who among them would beat
swords into ploughshares, and what language do
murderers cultivate in communicating to the other?

Isn't martyrdom then a little too convenient? that confronted
with the difficulty and hardness of living and
weighed by the burden of our flaws we
prefer to find meaning in leaving than living on,
and justify our giving this one life away for things like
country and God, which God gave us this life and this body
and thought we weren't deserving a more honorable one?
When did God think our lives were worth anything?
And if he thought they were worth exchanging, why
did he place us on the earth in the first place, and didn't reserve
us in heaven? We are not one hundred dollar bills,
we're pennies lost in the couch cushions of heaven,
though if we did have worth, he would put us to administering
his holy kingdom and not in leading amphibious assaults
or strapping ticking bombs onto our chests. And perhaps this
indicates there is no kingdom whatsoever, that
confronted with the lack of order and meaning in our lives
we instead envision an otherworldly palace with these things

and seeing death as the final frontier we assume
this ethereal castle must live in those veils and the entry
is the mere token of belief, for belief is worth nothing,
as much as we are worth, not comprehending that
the celestial gatekeeper wouldn't let us in because such
a beautiful and pure kingdom wouldn't allow a fuck-up like you
who didn't spend whatever small time he had on this earth
even attempting a rearrangement of his soul so as to be in accord
with this otherworldly place and the act of sacrificing
that life reeks entirely of a desperation unfitting,
upon which argument the gatekeeper turns us back, in chains
to hell, the same we wished upon our enemies, and the same
chaos and panic we always felt we were destined for and didn't say.

Judgment Day is every day. We find ourselves sometimes
in pockets out of time where we reflect if only partially
the gears of the celestial mechanism and our relation to it
and guess at our maker's judgment of us based on how we
judge ourselves, and in that pocket of suspended time
we conclude upon the incident of a speeding car
or a stray bullet or even a Steinway falling out of the sky
we could conclude nothing in our lives was worth it,
nothing redeems us, and hell is just the tomorrow
where we go on living in meaningless, worthless ways.
And that is of course why Judgment Day is speckled
with the white bodies of sinners looking heavenward,
the hordes of them looking fearful, hair streaming down and
unshaven, because we know there will be many;
and the elevated on Ascension Day, who could those fuckers
be, their features blurred and melted in the pillars of light?

93

This must be the loneliness of the I

Broch wrote so convincingly and horrifyingly

and tiringly about as if he tired

of entering other men's skeins and saw

in them nothing but screaming abysses

that neuroses and disappointments and shame

had deepened which would accept no

grace or mercy or forgiveness to fill

them in in the hopes of their finally climbing out

for if they did climb out and see themselves entire

they would see and would realize they're small,

and that they would rather end themselves and enter

the stream of all souls knowing that they

died a hole, but they had died large.

When I straddled the length of the Brooklyn Bridge and saw

myself diving headfirst into the glassy water and breaking

every bone on its cerulean breaks or I crossed the street wishing

some stray sedan would smash into me hurtling me some many

meters into the air landing me onto the asphalt in a bloody

broken heap or I held the edge of the knife against my

wrist and tested its sharpness and desired to see drops of

blood descend the roundness of my arm I conceived there

how much pain the act would cause me and how much fear death

occurring to me would inflict on me and then felt some relief

because the most painful and the most horrible death would absolve

me of the guilt I had for living so long as a violent, antagonizing

creature, and that he who killed himself was a purehearted

man with the dignity to end himself in the benevolent

realization he was a continuing cancer to the earth

on the mere folly of simply being alive and advertising
that being alive itself was okay.

Judgment Day is every day. We are always in
Walmart looking at other shoppers and we are always
on our couches watching the Big Game and we are
always on the street with a rain-flattened hat judging
ourselves through the objects around us, relating ourselves
to the world surrounding us and the values they seem to emanate
toward us, the single mother with three kids, scrolling through
her phone, the blob on the Rascal scooter, the beautiful people
in the advertisement, the man wearing expensive watches,
and then ourselves to the crooked branches of the tree
enduring this rain as they have done for countless centuries
and will continue to do, these all present arguments
to our very being and the how, why and what of our existence,
and to our coat's lapel we begin to growl over our small space
these ideas dare to intrude.
                    The heart of violence is
forcing a new world over our own world
and not as a superposition and as violent a clash
as the Chicxulub asteroid's that destroyed all the dinosaurs.
We are always holding ourselves in our hands
and the singular phenomenon that is the world seeks to destroy us.
Because words are inherently violent. By describing
they assert, and the assertion itself is in complete disagreement
with its negative and the non-assertion; an assertion
itself is a cancellation and a violent declaration against
what it asserts, and this is a pity to us, for we lay
sentimental value on our assertions. We feel correct in

concluding, we feel right in maintaining, we feel

surefooted in our belief, for without them we fear

no one will exchange our dollars for food, our coughs

will not go away, and our neighbors will not refrain from

looking at us crossly. Without our mechanism, our own

world, as it stands, why should we believe tomorrow will be like

today? and that yesterday worse than today on account

of our inability to encourage the machine? We need

tomorrow to be better than today, and we suspect

every word streaming from another's mouth is an evil

that turns our orientation ever so slightly away from the direction

the machine ordered us to.

                          Words have power. They are

palisades, they are caltrops, they are dragon's teeth

that we scatter across our soul to protect it from foreign influence,

the more the better, more is welcome, for the more involvement

we have with the machine the closer we become to it and entrenched

in its ways and the more it loves and rewards us through

subtle means, and the word is a spear and a sword too,

that by contrasting our world to another's we say,

this world is mine, it's better than yours, take a look at it

if you want to see what superiority looks like, but if you

find yourself too ashamed then stay out of it lest

I show you my ingenious defenses.

                          We scatter across our souls

the words of climate change, of family values, of diversity,

of Christianity, of liberty, of sanctity, in order to show

other people, back the fuck up from me.

Cain slew Abel. The victim

                      is the object of the sentence.

And when words are violent we can only share violence.

Yes...and though I abhor this to be true,
"God" is but a word, a most dangerous one at that.
"In the beginning was the Word, and the Word
was with God, and the Word was God."
The most dangerous weapon man ever made was the word.
Missiles do not fire themselves, atom bombs do not explode
but upon the words "fire" and "fall",
and the word "holocaust" like a horseman precedes fear.

"Country" is a dangerous word
people say while holding their hands
to their hearts. When they say "country"
they imagine an immense mother
whose breasts are heavy with milk
and whose hairs are ears of corn
and whose hands swat all danger
and that we must be grateful
as otherwise the soil will be dust
and plants will refuse to grow
and our children will not be as tall
or wise as their parents, or, worse,
obedient to us, and that enemies will
cross our borders, sneer, and raise
their rifles and fire at women, mostly,
whose duty is to resemble the "country"
and be as passive and receptive as she is.
And with "country" comes "history"
encompassing the "noble" acts done

on this country's soil or on behalf of her

as performed by some diligent "patriot"

as laying their lives to shoot at enemies

as laying their lives to guard from enemies

as laying their lives to delude enemies

and "enemy" is a dangerous word too

for upon waging it on Indian or socialist

or Japanese or African they

are rinsed of all their innocence and must

answer to the judgment of "country"

which is usually the barrel of a rifle

and however many "patriot" lives necessary.

And for all this gratitude and loyalty,

and for the privilege to say,

I am thankful everyday to have been born

in this country, to be privileged as to

participate on an earth so storied

with eminent personages, and to be

separated from those born to other

heathen "countries", such that I

cannot expect a dirtier, filthier existence,

the "patriot" is rewarded, every April,

by handing out their money to

a man who smilingly enters his door,

holds out his hand, and says, Gimme

or else I'll bring the men with guns.

"Government" is a dangerous word too,

wouldn't be so bad if it originated from "govern".

"Government" is but the lump that grows on

"country" that "patriots" must suffer

for believing in the word. "Government"
dresses in the mantle of "country",
assures us it participates in the shared
suffering and subsequent pride of "country"
and thus is entitled to the people's money.
"Government" confuses the concept
the people are stronger when sharing
with the concept, people are stronger through it,
"government". And if it were wise, the people
might actually buy it. Instead,
the "patriots" who defend "government"
impel the people to pay "government"
because they have to pay "government" too
and it's only fair we sink equally on a
sinking vessel, and drown.
Thus "government" is: "sunk cost fallacy".

And "church" is a dangerous word
whose "holy" men, its preachers and priests,
exhort the people to "peace", "generosity",
"virginity", "charity" and "family"
and then to close their eyes and
clap their hands together and suppose
a kingdom enrobed in light
and the light chiming of bells and that
they are within the border of this kingdom
now without their pain and deprivation
and never will they return to these
for this kingdom is accompanied with "all-knowing"
and "all-powerful" which essentially mean

"everything you are not and cannot conceive

but best believe I know more than you."

This kingdom is the dangerous word "heaven"

which the preachers and priests do not pretend

is real but subtly suggest it is more a state

of mind or else people ask "how" and "where"

otherwise known as "very good questions".

But these preachers and priests do not clarify

else how would "heaven" be used as a weapon

triggered by the words "sin" and "guilt"

on the day of paying tithes, for these words

conjure all the faults people have in them

and are aware constrain them and yet

these faults are absent from the people they pay.

And as for the word "pope", the master

of these priests and preachers, this is given

to the man who sees things as plain as

the leaves strewn on the brick path

the ripples made by birds on the waters

the whistle of the wind in the tree hollows

and shares these revelations with their flock

who listen, simply shrug their

shoulders and continue administering

to their flock which is to pass the plate

around for "donations", while their "pope",

withered dinosaur, sleeps a little,

dreams a little, and has a second helping of pasta.

And "science" is a dangerous word

supposing itself the opposite of "church"

unifying those under its banners of not

paying "church" any longer and instead

lining the pockets of "science" in order to build

respectable, noble and very expensive machines

which the scientists feed scraps of paper

supposedly containing the complexity of life

in characters and numbers and receive

for their tributes of data wisdom

described in these same characters and numbers

which evidently are atomic enough and

present themselves in enough permutation

to calculate the nature and trajectory of infinity.

Where "church" relies on "God" and "heaven"

"science" relies on "reason" and "God"

and "reason" to them is a noble and sacred process

cultivated and cherished by a string of wise men

over the centuries, for the centuries some time must

reveal their wisdom in the same vein

a government bond eventually becomes accessible

and these men must be wise for they

fill their minds and mouths with many words

hitherto unknown and could not be made up.

And "reason", this magical process

understood by the wise and intelligent few

who must therefore be elevated from the

masses, is this: when we do this, and that

happens, then we know that that happens,

and therefore we can build hardly understood machines

to make more hardly understood conjectures.

We marvel, our mouths wide open,

and then we pay out to "science"

to see more marvels, which the scientists say

have built buildings, have fed the many,

have cured the many, and have made us powerful,

though people still go hungry, though health

still is unanswered, though our lives

are largely separate from "science", to which

it replies, this is all because you

have not given us enough money.

I find often that "science" is synonymous with "church"

though they abhor the comparison and "reason" that

they are not identical and continue doing the same things.

"Education" rides on the coattails of "science".

"Education" is seen as holy and noble, whose columns

are made of alabaster, whose caryatids are maidens

with bare arms and pure and untouched

by the muck of "ignorance" which is often

the question "why", and this temple is veiled in a

mist whose dews are threaded by light, and who

is the origin of this light, but "God"? ("Country",

"church", "science", "education", they all

lay a claim on "God", and yet exult themselves

above the other.) "Education" is the older

generation teaching the newer old concepts

which is a bit like the robin chewing worms

in her beak before passing it onto chicks,

that is, what is passed down is not whole

but jumbled and piecemeal and thus apt

to confuse them. However, this suffices because

"education" has little to do with truth
but the instruction of "obedience" - that was
the heart of Plato's Republic, that children must
huddle, sit still, and stay quiet, and listen
to their elders hours of the day for the reason
that not protesting is a virtue and indicates
a heart that allows itself to be distorted
and even trampled over if this is required.
"Truth" is nice but "obedience" is better,
and the most obedient pupils are rewarded
and given unto higher institutions so that
they learn further reasons to not rebel
and do not question the ways of their superiors
and perform their actions which are chopped
up like the robin's worm so that the student,
or, acolyte, does not gleam the machine's design.
And to reinforce what the student does is good,
their attendance and scheduling has meaning
more than their willingness to be present in the machine
they are told they live in a "meritocracy", another
Platonic concept, meaning, absolute obedience
means the absolute good for the state
which has the effect of the students not examining
the conditions by which their fellows suffer.
I mean, who really cares?

And "society" is a dangerous word
accompanying the dangerous "meritocracy"
because it supposes itself the product of this
luminous, impeccable, entirely efficient machine

vouchsafed by the vision of the ages and should not

be questioned or else a wheel fly in fire

and the whole apparatus groans and shudders

falling down. "Culture" is a dangerous word

accompanying "society" denoting the

pretty phrases and pictures only the "sophisticated"

can understand and therefore attach ingenious

meaning onto, thus making these things prettier.

These pretty phrases and pictures replace the function

of words, such that they communicate meaning

with an immensely reduced palette of meaning,

which allows clever people to live their lives

with less thoughts. And to defend themselves from thinking

by those who explore the meaning behind words,

they have developed pretty defenses as "not hip to it",

"square", "not in style", "loser" and "incel".

And "beauty" is a dangerous word

often accompanying "culture", bestowed on

the paintings, music, literature supposedly fostered

by "culture" and describes, upon seeing these

words, the pinch and the squeeze of our bowels,

for "beauty" cannot be understood by our

rational powers and lies within the province of

the all-powerful "gut". "Gut" is a kind of sixth sense

that senses whether something is "beautiful" or not.

It has no other uses beyond this, though

this organ to some should be exalted above all,

in large part because a good deal of their income

derives from it. Note "gut" sounds like "God".

"Hierarchy" too is a dangerous word,

but I've already spent many thoughts on it –

it is, some for you and most for me, and,

the world must work this way, else it doesn't,

and that you are not high in it and

you should feel ashamed, and your ability

to feel shame means it is impossible

for you to be accepted.

And "chance" too is a dangerous word, not at all

related to the word "chaos", though it ought to be,

for "chaos" is confusing, it swallows all sense in

and we ought to be humble to it; "chance", instead, says,

all fortunes I have gained, are mine only,

which means I am exceptional, which means I

am favored by "God", which "chance" actually hides behind.

"Take a chance" means "hope God accedes"

and, "God" being gracious, we go

to Vegas, buy a boat, or seek clubs,

because having been graced by God means

there's not a bad "chance" God acquiesces again.

Though "chaos" too is a dangerous word, as

words can have many uses, and we

are able to apply innumerable improper uses

to any number of words. "Chaos" is often said

with a shrug when a plane crash, a power outage

or a wildfire occurs and takes however many lives,

which lives we throw into the whorl of "chaos"

when we say, What can be done? life is but "chaos".

"Chaos" accompanies the phrase, "things happen".

When it is said, we are given the fortune

of not thinking about it anymore, throwing our minds,

and, unburdened from responsibility, moving on with our day.

The invocation of "chaos" is a totem

we invoke when, for a short time, we do not

want to care about the consequences of our

actions, which is akin to throwing our lives away,

which is okay as life is not worth living,

at least, so "chaos" dictates.

And "death" is a dangerous word

for when one thinks "death" one imagines

chilling fogs and dark valleys teeming

with voracious animals, and elements

unforgiving and harsh, even though

true death is an absence of all feeling

and thus seems a refreshing change.

"Death" is often used in distinction to

"heaven" and is often employed by "church"

but death has acquired powers by the means

one enters it, as the shorting of one's

senses, the loss of life-sustaining blood,

or the destruction of the mind.

Because these means are violent-seeming,

one imagines "death" is a violent place,

although sometimes violent means elicit joy

as is the case for rollercoasters.

And so people dislike the word "death",

dislike to speak of the causes of "death", and

dislike even discussing people who have "died",

as otherwise, though they hate life,

"death" may ruin the regularity

of their normal routines.

And "happiness" is a dangerous word as well,

often used in distinction, or in defiance,

to "death", so that the goal of "happiness"

is to experience as much before entering the grave.

After that, there is no agreed-upon definition.

For some "happiness" is a good meal, others

it's a good lay, for others it's a child

on one's knee, for some, no children,

and to some it is to drive fast cars,

and yet these worshippers of "happiness"

hold their eyes aloft into the vaults

of "heaven" and praise

the great blessings of "happiness"

as if it has any power among them all.

Thus happiness is a fairly useless word

and accompanied by a shake and

nod of the head, meaning we are free

to discount another person's "happiness"

especially if it impinges on ours.

And "freedom" is a dangerous word too

for it denotes a state of being unrestrained

by the words aforementioned and unsaid –

and one is almost seduced by "freedom"

which evokes images of fine-plumed birds

soaring through wide and unbroken sky,

unpeopled vales and vast sea,

beneath only the twinkling stars,

until one releases "freedom", too, is a word

and words constrain. "Freedom" is only swapping

cages, and so "freedom" is nearly

meaningless, so some surmise the word

belongs only to the dead, who are truly

free from the restraints of our senses

and minds. Others define "freedom"

as amounting to the loosening

of the collar of one's workshirt.

"Freedom" is often associated with "free-thinking"

which, again, is like the tiger

pacing "freely" within the bars of its cage.

We cover ourselves in words and their systems

for, lacking meaning ourselves, we prefer to invent

things that have meaning, to delude ourselves

and our neighbors from seeing clear, because we

seek to gain something from it. When the black spires

of Babel were erected, Nimrod surmised man

was the operator of his destiny and sufficed

to replace God, and God laughed, his laughing

thunder sufficient to blow Babel down and in

its collapse scattered the settlements of men,

for it was just a tower. We gave power to the word

"tower" and then we said, because this is tallest,

it is the most powerful, and its maker more still.

But we made it. There are no "towers"

108

in the tapestry of existence. It may as well

have been made out of words, in fact that

is truly what it is made of, just words

that drove measly men to raise measly whips

onto measlier men to stack brick by brick.

And in the same sense, we are just words too,

we are inventions of ourselves, what we say concerning

ourselves is true, because it doesn't matter what we are,

as nothing shall verify or conclude who we are.

We stack delusions upon others, and we call this grand one

"life", and these delusions become gods themselves,

ones we pray to, hold ourselves to, and curse

others for disbelieving them, we exchange delusions

as currency, we suppose ourselves as having feelings

based on these delusions, and we feel pleasure

and censure on them too – until God laughs,

and we find ourselves at the bottom of belief

with no footing any longer for our souls to stand on.

We are all waiting for truth all our lives,

we are all waiting to wake up; we never do.

And "love" is a dangerous word too,

one whose many envoys as "marriage"

and "monogamy" I can paint, and whose

many stations and follies I can sing of,

but it suffices to say "love" is a delusion

to prevent our realizing on dry afternoons

that our lives are adrift on hollow words,

that we can only exchange words not our own,

and that we are horrifically alone.

And now I sing of the most dangerous word
that all the other words revolve around, "God",
a repository of many meanings, such as
"history", "virtue", "future", "justice",
"fortune", "happiness", "strength",
and because so many meanings accumulate into it,
it is nearly meaningless. "God" is a
censer one uses to perfume one's words
and actions, providing justification for them
amounting to "Because we cannot question
existence, for we simply are, I do
as I please" and rather than saying so plainly
we use "God" so as not to invoke
the is-ness of existence and thus question
the intricate system of words parasitizing
off this handwave of a word.
And we believe the handwave. Because
it doesn't matter. We can rationalize ourselves
ever and ever, try to understand our place
on this world and our feelings and our
experiences, juxtaposed to the
urgency of time and the inanity
of the grave, and we can invent
explications for the intensity of our
emotions and our presence in this world,
and yet we will always be keenly aware
none of this matters, and whatever
meaning we try to deploy migrates
to the vacuum of all meaning.
And this, is "God". Adam once saw

the world as sufficient to live in

for it was made precisely for him to live in,

and when he tasted of knowledge he

learned of the idea of meaning,

but he did not know what the relation

between himself and all things meant,

why "taste", why "sight", why "sensation",

and so from a garden of all delights

where one was complete with the garden

and the garden was complete with one,

he fell into a world of disparate thoughts

and sensations and names and in the multitude

became lost, unable to find himself again.

"God" is the word for that which we lost,

our relationlessness to the world, or,

the non-existence of existing.

Ah, the darkness of hell.

That means I've dived deep.

That means there is only a little

distance remaining to the hole

of hell where I won't see

the whiteness of my hands and

feet nor the light of my soul.

There is no God.

I hesitate to say this

because then there is no reason

for men not to hurt

for men not to wound

for men not to lie

for men not to kill

their fellows, and me.

Yet, what law? what fear?

of what punishment?

for their own good?

You can't name

a million evils

done every day?

What justice?

What reason?

These have no

material form

but slaughter does,

massacre too.

If there is no

guarantor of

goodness then

goodness simply

is not.

These are all but words

we scream into the void

and the void answers not.

Nothing answers.

And there is nothing.

Down of heart, be glad:

Without goodness,

there is no badness.

Without charity,

there is no greed.

Without love,

there is no hate.

In the absence of all

all is rinsed

of their evils

because absence says

we are not real,

none of these thoughts

are real and shortly

we will not be real

on a point

in space we can

easily erase. And if

we amount to nothing

then words

amount to nothing

and what only suffices

in describing our

existence is

silence.

Silence.

Silence.

Silence.

Yet this too is too much.

I descend.

II

So that you, darling, grow pale on your pallet

(your rushes, your reliquary, your Golgotha),

and what merit your wan? like lilies, like snow, like

spilt milk, like sea spume, like eiderdown, like pages

falling of their book, to fall upon life's

cruelest hook that warmth you richly prized,

the ruddiness of your cheek as mantlepiece stood,

and your breath's heat ebbs away which you had struck

like a pin, and you don't begin, dear darling, to chase

after, speak towards, countenance a look at it, denounce

instead at wit's end your fingers clattering upon your

lap curses deserving for that sailor boy, head full of

book, that yellow-bodied pig whose notions are stuck,

and what will I do with you, my darling, warming

my coat, ingle-isled, ice clustering my throat of the

moon's solitary defile, whistling penitences amid the storm

and already borne of your death is a reeking, mild odor,

aroma of decay, that pummeling pride which stood to be

honored a different day becomes the Pyrrhic sword decried,

now drops and shatters you into fodder. Shall any other

gentlemanly whisk you away? So come now, white darling,

as the flies wag their beaks and river out your eyes

and holler down the streets of your breasts' incline,

and from the savage scene we sail starless night and

aqueous moon, and my sighs enlidding a pail

of Empyrean's poorest fools I guess at the vastness of experience, no, its torturous dreamings, this paltry human seeming

as I gut you with my knife so that your soul spills

from the wound, falling of your feet and to that final tomb,

the afterlife, only life that could be real, though my father likes

to invent all these various sentiments and feelings

that humans make their battlement of wisdom; the body, I discard;

the jokes of greatest temptation are those of transfiguration as reward,

and I can't help but ask, no, I can't help myself,

I can't help but ask aloud

Why does Man struggle?

So I asked thence I was born, for I knew

all things always, I knew I was to be born,

I was impatient, I wanted to do and do superlatively,

for how could humanity Die if there was no Death?

preposterous, and that my father, God, delayed my birth

by my mother, Beauty, well, absurd, obscene,

ignorant and headless, and my mother was heavy

with birth when three fellows with gilt crowns

saw the star of my birth high in the ovulating

sky and stole them to the manger where my mother

kicked her legs up in anticipation, I presume,

I decided not to look out, for post-Death,

the world will never be the same again, so what

was a few seconds more to me? I was ready

to govern life, my father said, you are the governor

of life, ensure all have an ID, and when

they leave take this ID and make certain they never

return back, and no one may duck the law,

no matter how troublesome they are, for Man

is your servant and you are a servant to Man;

fair enough, and I wanted to bellow from

my mother's cunt, Eldest man! Sickliest man!

fear me not, you who are so awfully old,

and so abhorrently infirm, you I will take

first, than the ones after you, the Neanderthals,

the Nephilim, the Aesir, the Atlanteans,

but for now I busied myself with my window

and my cupboard, my tea kettle and my ingle,

for gods came to do obeisance to me; Pain

was there, so was Suffering, and Agony,

Angst, Depression, Hopelessness, Suicide and Oblivion;

and their feet trampled over that cowardly

sniveling Life; they hailed and praised me, for I

was master of them all, showered them with

lessons, benedictions and prayers, and when I heard

a trumpet roar in the sky, splitting the heavens

in so immense a thunderburst, I folded the hut,

the cupboard, tea kettle, shooed away those

insufferable brothers and kicked out Life,

and as I raced out my father lovingly set a sign

in the sky, streaked with red, bursts of embers,

and I came out fully realized, crying to the North:

The final flowers shall honor my feet, from now

until the end of time! and to the West:

I am the greatest of gods! Thou hast worked

toward me; toil no longer, supreme that I am,

final that I am! and to the South:

I am unequal to all, I am unworthy of all!

I shall be the last one standing! and to the East:

Empty Gaia, beteem you of my offerings!
then to my Father: never more blessed and praised
have you been, now I have urged out of your head!
And shepherds and angels alike came to witness
my wailing, and they bowed before me
and received my blade between their eyes,
and blood gushing from their brows they cried:

O wise one, scion of beauty, endless virtues illuminate you!
Surely you will slay everyone and therefore impart meaning,
for all the cattle in their souls comprehend
that Death regenerates grief and suffering!

With rays of love light the world, peerless one,
make certain you spare no expense of your gift;
your fury transcends all fury,
with your might, roar, rend this delicate world!

And I overcome Charlemagne, I overcome Alexander,
I overcame Attila, and I overcame Joan of Arc,
I hungered over Hannibal, and Genghis I gnawed on,
I made minced meat of MacArthur, sauce of Scipio,
I pulped Pol Pot, made him into juice,
and Saladin I diced into salad, and Hitler
I developed a hankering, having made honey-glazed
ham of him, and Washington I whetted on
having mixed him into wontons, and I kneaded
Grant into graham crackers, and of Caesar
of course I cooked into dressing and drizzled him
over the the bacon of Napoleon's body,

and Mao was a mouthful – rolling

on his death bed his white wide body,

his two fillets of hair and the depression of his cheeks,

who as a revolutionary reacted as gave him success

in his lifetime: he raised and pointed his gun

at me, he shouted and shot in the hope

that I would, of the foundations of his empire,

be one more body buried beneath its pillars,

but I laughed, swallowed his bullets between my teeth,

and he cried, for he convinced himself even to the end

that he would be immortal – immortal! I laughed,

did you think rattling your saber would intimidate Death,

did you think acting the tiger would make you any less

human, and that by being inhuman evade me?

but so you know, the great and the peasants

have the exact same thought – and those you have ended,

by sword or by famine, they go down all the same,

so flashed I my great dogtooth and pierced deep

into the central sulcus, and he screamed all the while

he ranged down the shadow of the valley of me,

and I laughed, and do wonder, what goes on

in the heads of these men, when they, with a word,

erase another's existence, through blade or bullet,

do they see themselves as the cause, or do they think

that, having seen bloodshed and skulls, death

is not *true*, that the bodies lie unbreathing

and can and someday will dance again? and yet

don't they understand that death lies with me,

and that, in their demands, I happily accede?

as, I don't jot down debts, I don't believe in barter,

death is for all – death is indiscriminate – I am final,
and I pondered a lot what to do with this chinese soldier,
who aspired to be a god, told everyone as much,
and made him into braised pork belly – stuff he ate so
much of, and the same he denied others,
and I made schnitzel of Xuanzong, meatballs of Mandela,
Jefferson into jam, and Gandhi into ghee,
I mixed Bismarck into Bisquick, and Bolivar into baloney,
Thatcher seasons tea, and Churchill is charcuterie,
Franklin froths coffee, and Mansa Musa must be
matzah, Catherine makes good barbecue, and Phillip
serves as fillets, Roosevelt, a roast,
and the Claudians were like an assortment of chocolates
suited to my taste, Augustus, Tiberius, Caligula,
Claudius and Nero, and the line after
David, Solomon, Rehoboam, Abijah,
too long to list, were like a long advent calendar
whose panels were the visages of sweet babes,
a long month where every day was Christmas,
and Man puts a lot of stock on Adam, but
Eve sinned first, birthed first, died
first-ish, a Triple Crown winner of failure,
birthed the first murderer too, Cain, whom
my father set aside for me like a treat
tucked away in the lunch box, I loved them
all, patriarchs, statesmen, leaders of countries,
like the Huns, the Romanovs, for they were
little promises of more people, of a future
never growing stale, their preserving their kin
only so that they may one day die, delighted

120

me, even when they lambasted me, claimed
they defeated me, but a little longer living
doesn't make me blanch, snow white my bones
already are, instead it makes me salivate,
and so I said to Anastasia, who escaped from
the bloodbath, you can run and run, on horse
or on steamer, you'll be in my arms and
consummate with me, someday soon,
and he reminded me of a marshmellow
on a stick, presented to a campfire, Christ,
at the end Muhammad was as red as a
pomegranate, Moses, on Mount Nebo, thought
I wouldn't walk so far for him, but everywhere
is a good place to die, and the Buddha
had the sly idea that he wasn't evading
me, but taking departure of all life –
I thought the idea was cute and gave him credit,
but I slurped him down all the same,
and the Resurrection is really a retch,
the transmigration, tripe, Jannah, a joke,
I adore the "metaphor" but there's very much only me,
yes, just me, no gates of gold on fluffy white clouds,
no seventy-two virgins, no thousands of realms,
no rays of light, and no meeting the wise men past –
it's just me, I put you in your proper place,
I tie you up and leave you in store
as if sealing you in Ziplock bags, so to save
you later for future savoring, and that's all
you and your loved ones amount to, regardless
of what pulses run through your head at the time

I arrive, you're all just little tastes for me,

and Dr. King, I washed down with Dr. Pepper,

Luther I rinsed with Rémy Martin, and Augustine

went down well with asparagus, Plato, pâté,

Hobbes was an hors d'oeuvre for Rousseau

who made a good roux, Voltaire was vinegar,

Marx a meringue, and Aristotle good risotto,

smartasses all – I thought these eggheads

would be too yolky for my liking, they tried

arguing with me, not that I didn't exist

but that there had to be more to life,

and I made a face, and said, There is nothing more

to life, what, did you think you'd

get the girl at the end, life is anticlimatic,

get over it, I didn't write the script,

your great grasp of reason, your honed sense

of intellect, those *might* come from a great

consciousness, yes, you want answers and

answers, but who doesn't want to know,

and, frankly, you don't need to know,

you go down all one way, all the same,

and you've no one to blame but yourselves

for even spending so much time and energy

getting worked up over absolutely nothing,

seriously, I hate these smart people, who think

there's any use bargaining with me, and that's why

I savaged Salk, put a saddle on 'em and barked for a ride,

whipped him, kicked him, bespectacled puke,

Nightingale I rendered naked and ordered her to sit

on my scythe, the head of Hippocrates I cracked

122

flogging him much in my pleasure, and Fleming

I set aflame using but a fart and a lighter,

and Koch I really disliked, caught him in a vice

and kept him crushed in it as one of his vials,

and Edison was easy, I simply shoved

a bulb in his ass, and saw a light through his mouth,

Curie I carved and asked if she were atomic yet,

Einstein, white-headed, I ended by halving

his corpse and flinging them into the reaches

of the world, and wondered at their relative places,

and Newton I simply dropped – and heard

his scream echoing from the dark, until he hit the rocks,

I really can't stand these sirs and madams who try

to push me back, put me a little back, think in their minds

they are setting me ever so slightly aside, and soon

someday I won't even be a question,

I liked to tug their ears and cry, Am I

so reasonable to you, can my vastness

be contained by any-sized brain, can my

phenomenal being be rationalized with, so I had

to remind them they were bodies still, bodies

after all, and their matter wouldn't mean anything

even with medicine and machines, and that

adding just a bit more comfort into life, only made me

rage all the harder and greater, and at least

Donne said, Death be not proud, and Hesiod

gave me my formal honors, Dickinson received me

with solemnity, and Thomas told others to not

go silently into me, and Porter praised my

inevitability, and the Egyptians flattered me by

123

writing a whole book about me, though the Greeks

had Heracles wrestle me – see, this is why

the Greeks can't have anything nice, how could I

spare their civilization after that – and Beard

tried to flatter me, drawing me overpowering a tiger,

Böcklin drew me with violin, didn't know I took lessons,

and Klimt respected me, depicting me quite creepy,

at least artists like me, don't try to subvert me,

understand how singular I am – for a world

with death is simply not like any other world.

And listen, without me, there would be no Madonna,

there would be no Elvis, or Brando, or Divine,

or Chaplin, Laurel and Hardy, Dean,

and you bet Hepburn and Marilyn wouldn't be around,

because when I'm present, mankind needs a distraction –

and I welcome all your entertainers, who are like

dancing piles of meat to me, for when I am weary

and must put my sickle down, I watch me videos

in the cold extremes of the world. I would have killed

for a cameo in Thriller. Next time, then.

What does Man need in the presence of so eminent

a person as I? What astrology, what credit card,

what God Save The Queen, what Flag Day,

what Sheol, what Pax Romana, *ding an sich*,

Epicureanism, Cubism, or recipe

invented by what bag of blood, is more than my reality?

Whether the sun comes up or the moon comes down,

I will be your friend, and your children's, and theirs too,

I am your neighbor's aspiration, when traffic is long,

when the in-laws are in town, when

he is passed over by promotion, and yours too,

yes, doesn't everyone want to be me, Death,

escorter from this world to no other, remover

of complainers and cripples, the homely and the homeless?

And when you are but a twinkle in the eye

of history, which is no history at all

for Time does not count its years, in fact tomorrow

is no different than today, is no different than

a millenium ago or the days before Earth,

know that I will still be alive, humming, waiting

for my Father to make humans all over again,

so I can whet my appetite on them again.

But,

    Achilles, Hector, Paris; Paris, Hector, Achilles;

these names ring in my head, not all the time,

but every so often in chimes, they sing through

the throbs of me, and in my immortality I shouldn't

be attached to some motes of dust, but

Achilles, Hector, Paris, again. I suppose even the gods

have favorites. Yes, Paris, Hector, Achilles,

there Thetis threw her arms upon his corpse,

stripping him of ingenious armor; Hector,

blood streaking on the dirt in striped trails;

Paris, eye full of arrow; and then that day

like a lyrical dream sung out of a boy's mouth

who performance end fell down and died,

and now,

        Agamemnon, Menelaus, Ulysses,

Locrian Ajax and Diomedes, Andromache

and her virgin girls weeping, weeping over Hector's

overstrained carcass, Priam at his wine,

the forest is unstirred, no longer crackling with

a thousand torches, no tents are hoisted up,

armor is no longer slung on the ground,

and Scamander slumbers on the rocks,

banners are unfurled, battlements are abandoned,

and sentries have rolled their staves away,

the stars twinkle, laying bare orphans and widows,

emptied ships, catapults, stores, and me

on the moon, sickle-eyed as always,

watching once more Sinon, Laocoön, Cassandra

grind her teeth and gnaw on her fingers,

for who, of them, had the bitterest fate?

The direction of the wind, the wine

in their guts, the warmth of the night,

I remember it all, I do, I must be spurred

by the song, well, play on, boy,

                              play

that first crash, almost accidental, a sound

transcendental and fleeting, the first unwarlike

pot or pan bashing or bridle lashing and lacerating

the stoic air boorish with peace, yes, at so much ease,

infeasible would flames and blood be, and yet

raining from the battlements, epistrophy,

pleading, begging, whining to God, as good as whimpered

to a pile of clod, the Achaeans blast the walls with

fire and blood, bespattering the stone, singeing

the wood, and here a man's brains burst, there

another's fly, Ajax carves holes in his crown,

126

then over the wall he winds, and, oh,

shall so many good things happen to me? I think, as I

were a czar, an earl, a prince? tender and raw

are my skin, struck through the hands and breasts

with pins, love and hate give to haranguing men?

destined Menelaus, let the missiles play a requiem

for your brothers upon the bridal gown, swing

left, swing right, cleave the enemies' crowns,

wine skeins and gloves out of bloodied scalps,

your Helen in her spire, where Pyrrhus raves onward,

his father's spectre hound hungry prisoned in impossible tower,

but first, the overture: hopeless they wail

as the gates clatter groundward like coins and what flows

are those murderous men and their tools

hugging their hips, sweat on their brows,

and wine on their lips and braid on their heads and carnage

on the tips of their cunt-born minds, kill is their soul

and something like this unfolds: ants wrenching the limbs

of a stray freshly slaughtered, taking this and that,

plunging their pincers in without falter until

the whole piece unsolders, unrecognizable

now, chunks and bits left over or taken into tow,

now reveal the ants as heroes, their cargo

women and children, beaten black and blue,

mewling, defenestrated, their loves and their fathers

lying on the ground, after "valiant struggle", oh play,

play on boy, as the flames topple the cupolas,

ornamented cherubs, shingles alike, Priam trapped

in his estate on the edge of a knife upon Pyrrhus's

coming, battle-ax ready, and were there

notions wide and heady streaming from his mouth,

for the sake of his family, wife and girls, any

homilies to save the souls of his sons-in-laws and boys,

any wily fable to reprimand the maniac? None –

only swears, insults, finally tears as his head tumbles

down – Pyrrhus with one arm plies Andromache down,

down that last citadel of Ilium goes,

down Cassandra's face is pushed to the dirt, to the altar

she goes, and did she pray to Pallas, did Pallas

watch, did she send Pegasus, nobody knows,

oh, I'm not worthy, what is our Mother Earth to me,

the fires and entrails burning, what is this all to me?

but that these men sweat for *me*, they gnash for *my*

sake, they spare neither young nor aged for the fear

of my vengeful hands, over land and sea people sweat

for me – in the night, in their cold, in their hallways

wrapped in robes – so they plunder, why wonder?

so Ajax ruptures that white wall, his thigh

there blood falls, they maim, desecrate gods

not their own, pilfer, break eyes set like stone,

and shaking the vaults of heaven let out my mighty

roar winding through the air in a spiral tour

and igniting greater flames and blood-cries in its course

all the way to the killing floor, guttural it came out,

riotous and pleased, annunciated then crucified,

now shrieked at the earth's cunt, swollen

with abortive deeds, my eyes weep with blood,

breathing heavy underneath me a million

hands bolster me up, proclaiming me as God –

light and limpid, how could I tell them off? Father!

thou with me be not covetous, it's Man

who wants a a god, a god of blood,

Ulysses stealing the god's likeness, horses

slashing the air, eating the butchery off the floor,

Diomedes's mares, and what does Cassandra see?

wide-eyed and bare to the waist, face covered

in curls: Clytemnestra, her death, or perhaps

blood for blood the daughter, Thetis's son, or

the boy love? Or the countless bodies sinking

slowly in the wine-dark waters or the children

whose inheritances lie wasted without their fathers,

and Menelaus looks up, the mirror in view –

he sees not himself, he sees two, three, four,

countless of bested Greeks ascending higher

upon the steps of a Byzantine tower, and sees

something else, he doesn't know what it means,

it's not the moon nor the knife nor his hard-won queen,

no, nor the fuming heap, it's Death, great Death, I supreme.

Now

that the moon is full

the cup is full the fire ful

some on the hearth recall

the days passed

over

placed in my mouth

the moon on my tongue

there's a hole in my teeth

showing my lungs

my my my

days done by

And now, a fable: a man passed through a waste

and saw a body lie. He made a great cry

for he saw the man had died. A man with a silver staff

came by, and he asked him who should bear the curse.

The man replied: God, the murderer, and travelers each

and every one will be eaten by the same worms

when all is said and done.

                And so I say

I earn all my fun

                whether man's follies run.

You all are the same worms when all is said and done.

Galop Infernal

The God of death lives like a lord at the bottom of hell.
Not for nothing Plato says "his name means the giver
of wealth, which comes out of the earth beneath."
The balustrades of his mansion were long, its corridors
sumptuous, its lattices luxurious, its eaves tall,
its columns high, and the authors of his books were erudite.
The whole affair was very tacky. I don't want to talk about it.
But it was funny and briefly touching.

                                  The Furies raised a
rancor over my invitation. "What! A human enter,
with unshod feet, into this sacred temple?" Imagine me,
having walked all the way down – believe me, hell
is very long – tired and dirty, making a face at these snaky
women, Allecto, Megaera, Tisiphone. They argued for dignity,
they argued for purity, they argued for precedent. What!
Everyone in that manor but I was a demon, some deranged
thing hated by God or at least given a cold shoulder. Denying me
is like the ribeye condescended by the rump steak.
It was hard to believe, not because I've been through every door,
but because my back was groaning, and going back up
was not in my imagination. But the lord of that hole refused
their generous disinvitation, and they glowered at me
all night. Whenever I noticed they were grinding
their teeth over me, I quickly glanced away and minded myself,
and a solicitous someone said, They don't like you.

The truth is that demons are not too interesting. Suffering
in general is not very interesting. It's certainly very sad,
but it's not exactly for table talk, and when your aunt
complains the ATM does not let her withdraw, you pay
more attention to your meal. And that's all they do,
they cause suffering, because they suffered all.

They're messes. They're fodder for Freud. He would
have had a field day with them. For instance, one of them
whips poor souls for a living. He knows his work well,
he knows how to twist his wrist, he knows when
in the arc to lash, he knows where it stings and scars,
and he knows when they've had enough, to give
over to his colleagues to stick candles up their ass.
Now, don't call me a heartless fellow for saying
I'm unsympathetic, I hardly know these people;
surely you don't know all about your neighbors, though
you share sugar with them. Anyway, he serenades us
as we eat our meal – roast pygmies, men a la mode,
women pregnant and engastrated – and suddenly
this man gets himself heavy and expounds how
he whips himself in the evening and doesn't flinch, so
to know how his sufferers feel and so to see himself
as superior to them, and now we're comforting the fellow
as he bursts into tears and soothing him with the assurance
he is doing a good job. I sit there and think,
Who finds so much meaning in their job?

In the case of a succubus, she hemmed and hawed
on her prowess to seduce men, and then supposed

132

her sexual abilities were to persuade them on the straight
and narrow; and I think, Who finds so much meaning in sex?

And don't get me started on incubuses. Everyone thinks
their lives must be affirmed, because their primary feed
is women. But these fellows are sulky. Some
struggled on the down payments of their car, and some
had wives who disapproved almost every facet of their job.

And one of them was named Pazuzu; he was mighty
upset that he never received proper royalties
for being in The Exorcist, and whenever
he worked the nerve to call Friedkin about it,
his children would ask him what that movie is,
and he would then be too depressed to go through with it.

Only Beelzebub seemed to feel sufficiency.
Every now and then he sat down with a cup of soup,
asked for the chef, and pointed to a fly in the minestrone.
He tells me he has never failed to get a refund.
He says the cooks of Midtown are getting suspicious,
but, he reasons, who on earth can summon flies willy-nilly?

And my God do demons like bad jokes:

Why did the dead baby cross the road?
Because it was nailed to the chicken.

Knock, knock.
Who's there?
Dead baby.

Dead baby who?

But she had long left.

Roses are red,

violets are blue,

and so are your eyes

and dead babies too.

Jack and Jill went up the hill

to fetch a pail of water;

Jack fell down and broke his crown,

a dead baby by his father.

How many dead babies does it take to screw in a light bulb?

God forbid we let them get cold.

A dead baby walks into a bar.

The priest, pastor and rabbi were just done with him.

As you can see, demons like dead baby jokes.

Don't shoot me, I'm just the poet.

When dinner ends, the tables are turned,

a crowd forms, and the dancing begins

though demons don't dance. They plod.

But the Furies

        dance.

           They Charleston.

Shake.

     Mash Potato.

        Mazurka.

Twist.

    Watusi.

        Tango.

            Time Warp.

Though everyone claimed the Furies were teetotalers

and never had a draught since they were seed,

tonight they inhaled barrelfuls of wine

and, more than tipsy, clearly flushed, bobbing

their heads, as if they were adrift on water,

pointed their fingers at me, the object of their unction.

Allecto spoke first, foremost of the sisters:

"Loutish poet, skimmer of the upper world,

do you know who we are? We are called Kindly Ones

but we're not known for being nice. No, when men

talk big and fail to meet their obligations, whether to

parent or wife or child, we torment them,

we put bags of dog poop on their stairs and

set the dog barking with rubber snakes.

"So it is in all the heavens. The chthonic gods

exist for one reason: to make man's life

inconvenient. When someone steps out

of line and makes life easy, we intervene,

for what have men done for us to be generous?

"So it goes

        with wise Prometheus,

Iapetos's son, he of the shimmering mind,

135

when he surveyed all on earth's surface
and saw only man's woe, his powerlessness
in growing crops tall and keeping warm in howling
nights, and, concerning himself with other
people's affairs, furnished him with fire.

"For this he was chained to a rock
and, every fortnight, an eagle espies
him, wretched thing, and plunges his beak
into his liver, rips it out like a belt.
Then the storm lord wings away, letting the wound fester,
then, to heal, all so the noble animal can do it again.

"So you see, those who are too clever
and don't respect time-honored traditions
have their livers ripped out, I suppose."

I shrugged my shoulders and replied,
"I'm not setting up a barbecue here."

This incensed them. Megaera pushed her aside
and began speaking in a rumbling voice:

"You know, your benefactor, Pluto,
the man whose power protects you as guest
and whom you rely on for blessings,
is wedded to a wife, it is true,
though she is not here now. Isn't that curious?

"His wife's name is Prosperpina and she
is the daughter of Ceres, giver of wheat

136

and gay song in the spring. The lord
of the dead snatched her, his niece, from
the home of her mother, leaving behind
a stinking crater at the scene of his rape."

The demons wished she used a softer word.
She called them idiots, and she resumed:

"And so every six months Ceres weeps
and the earth grows cold and snow
covers the field, and all life lies in grey.
But because she is with her mother now,
green covers the earth and the birds sing song.
So what do you think, knowing that your host
is a rapist and a pedophile?"

I thought it was odd that she still came back here
so I shrugged my shoulder and said "Love is love",
in part because I truly believe this and in part
I thought it was the politically correct thing to say.

Now it was Tisiphone's turn to speak,
and she began telling me off as her sisters did:

"That's enough insolence from you. Do you not recall
we are gods? Are you not aware one pays dearly
for being so defiant against their superiors?

"Marsyas too defied the gods, he challenged
Phoebus, the origin of music, to a duel,
and when he lost, as was bound to happen,

the mighty god skinned him, every inch
of flesh, and made him into a carpet.
The satyr looked like a rotisserie
and cried when the rain struck his body
and the salt of his tears hurt him more.
Now, do us honor, and make
like a tree, and leave this realm!"

Yet I could not hear her, indeed I could not
see any of them anymore, they diminished in the back
of the crowd forming around me, and they, so small,
scoffed, attended their dregs, and I know not
what happened to them, perhaps they hitched a ride home.

But the crowd looked at me with wide
eyes and large grins on their faces, and their
smiles seemed to be that of the wolf's
before he dines on some doe's meat, for the
invocation of flesh in the last story excited them.
I tried to make myself small, less bony,
less tender and less chewy; I thought of
excusing myself to the restroom, really, I had
a nose to wipe, some crusting eyes, and
I drank much more than I could hold.

But a dark figure passed through them – it was
the lord of the dead, stoic and somewhat grey,
and people departed not for his reputation
but because it was weird to see him
after he had been called so many names.

When I apologized on behalf of the Furies, he

shook his head and shrugged, and said,

They tell me this all the time.

                    Some people

are always as miserable as their minds are.

And the god of wealth imparted me with wisdom:

Mind what people say half of the time with half a mind.

And after the party,

                    the guests departing,

and catering received their checks,

                    he brought me

down to his vaults, bulging with all

the wealth of the world, a genuine

Mickey Mantle bat, an earring

Hatshepsut wore, a lost

episode of Leave It to Beaver,

Obama's birth certificate, the car

Princess Diana crashed, a signed

copy of the Odyssey, the sword

Cato disembowelled himself, Sima Qian's

balls in a goblet of Henry VIII's,

Archimedes' bathtub, and Taft's too,

Michael's glove, his chimp as well,

the original Lassie

stuffed, Ben Franklin's kite,

Washington's teeth and codpiece,

the Holy Grail, the Sword

of Damocles, the Ark

of the Convenant, and Carmen Sandiego,

and there is Pirithous, moored to his chair,

for the crime of fishing for another man's wife,

forever his boner stiff as him too,

and amid all these hoards he asked me,

As my honored guest, and frankly

I don't often entertain guests as you,

ask of me anything that is mine

and you shall receive it, and I

responded, I would like Eurydice.

He groaned and grimaced, and said,

Well, I don't have that. I rejoindered,

But you are king of the dead.

That's like asking Nixon for Utah,

he snapped, it's just a title,

I just happen to be responsible.

Do you not do anything at all?

Yes! And it's a great gig! Now look here,

how about Sasquatch's merkin?

I came all the way down this godforsaken place

and endured your truly awful dinner

just so you could tell me a week too late

I can't have Eurydice back? and he said,

You're right! And here are Marilyn Monroe's bloomers!

I don't have use for any of this shit!

And I huffed, turned and intended to storm home,

throw myself into warm water, and the toaster too,

when he said, There are rules to these things,

I can't just give her to you willy-nilly!

Dead is dead, dude, what, if I

snap my fingers, how will she return?

with a raspberry for an eye, or her breath

altered into a fart? I don't know!

The raspberry is fine, the fart, you can keep her.

What I mean is, I don't know what will happen.

I don't make the rules here. As they say,

Sir, this is a Wendy's. And I stood there

and blinked and acted a bit dumb, and I said,

Well, let's just see, and he said, What?

I said, Why don't we find out what happens?

What have I to lose, what do I live for?

And he gave me a long look, and said,

Fine, just go back the way you came,

she'll be there with you, and don't come back again.

And on his door he flipped

                              a Sorry, We're Closed sign.

And No Dogs Allowed, I'm not sure why.

Now, none of that happened, or at least

I *think* it didn't happen, it appears to me

now as a kind of dream, but aren't

dreams themselves touching and moving things?

It was all a metaphor for something, and, anyway,

you've only yourself to blame for listening to it all.

Notwithstanding, and nevertheless,

                              I ascend.

Song of my life

"Why don't you get a new girlfriend?"
That's an idea. I should have thought of that first.
But I've gotten this far, there must be some reward,
right? That's totally how it works.
Honestly, even I don't know why
it has to precisely be Eurydice,
or why it has to precisely be me
saddled with all of this bullshit.

What does it matter? I walk all the same.
I've been walking all my life. Alone
I've walked all my life. Whether
Eurydice is up there or not, I keep
on walking. Though now, I am very tired.

My worst enemy
                is myself.
"Who goes there? none else by;
Richard loves Richard; that is, I am I."
It's me battling me,
                and I'm losing,
or putting up a really bad fight,
or all I'm good for is getting in my own way.

Okay dude, who seriously wants to listen to you
bitch all the time? Right here, right now,

with all the time the stars provide, nothing better

doing, think of just one good thing about yourself.

"Man is the measure of all things,

alike of the being of the things that are,

and of the non-being of the things that are not."

I don't align Protagoras's saying with Plato's

interpretation, that all meaning is relative.

What beholds the world is our mind.

Nothing else on this earth is like it, nothing

shimmers and shines as it does, and puts

the world into so much rhymthic prose.

The eye sees, the mind measures,

and in measuring, assigns value to things,

on the foreground of our relation to them.

We create scales and rulers and meters

to put the properties of things into words,

thus making them more phenomenal, not less,

more special and more unique, and ourselves

ever more special, in our relation to them.

And if we find our instruments are wrong,

or we see something beatific in a new idea,

we change our measures and create new instruments.

And because we are gifted with thoughts

conceiving existence and non-existence,

as in, we conceive combinations and permutations

hitherto unseen and reason what is not

to bring attention to what is, we are

able to paint a picture of the world,

and even if this picture is incomplete

our painting allows us to be close to the earth

that is painting a picture of us

by the mere fact that it is. Therefore

we arrive to a kind of harmony with the earth

the more we come to learn and understand it.

Thus we are the measure of all things,

and we are free to make measures useful to us

and redefine measures obsolete to us,

as wisdom, as kindness, as justice,

so that they are attuned to the fact of living.

And that's why I believe

                       in astrology.

It's such a sad constituent of my being.

And the years run through a cycle of twelve,

the end of the cycle is not death and the start not new,

but merely an indication of some change

for we shall live through every life and fortune

of every kind before we enter our dying.

The rat starts the cycle, describing a being

first at the crack of dawn to scurry and search

after their next meal, and to lick the faces of its

brood clean. To many he's a lowly animal, because

he is a creature small and often unseen. I say

their view of life is too small. Where we

grumble incessantly the air is too cold or too hot,

find the world too large and horrible, and shield

ourselves in small houses, the rat finds the world

144

is too small to house its desire for living.

Those born in the year of the rat, then,

have a peaceable disposition, and yet a

craving to experience life, in small things

and large. All kinds of life like them

even though they are sometimes too quiet

and more anxious than others like. I find

they have a greater fear of death – they

banish mention of it, prefer it unreal,

an allegory, not a reality. Thus they

love life a little too much and have special attachment

to material things, and romanticize all

memory. Sometimes they see matter more than men.

But it's nice to know someone who lives in the moment.

Tolstoy and Hobbes, Shakespeare and Du Fu

and you, Bill, are rats. In Tolstoy there is

the mirth in scenes teeming with life,

in Du Fu there is urgency in keeping our life.

Next in the cycle is the ox, a slow and laboring

animal, surefootedness and stubbornness

in paradoxical measures, but when

he sees straight, no one can set him aside.

Of course, seeing straight is the hard part.

Sometimes these fellows are the worst of the world,

but I bet you can name a few

worth more than the treasures on this earth.

Those born in the year of the ox then

are quiet in action and solitary

and like to plop down on that which they adore,

whether it is their partner, happy living,

or the path of righteousness. They, more than rats,

can love things too much, and can lose

sight of reason for the sake of sentimentality

and oftentimes their own selfishness, so as

to be as blind as a raging bull.

Dante and Thoreau, Yeats and Wittgenstein

are oxen. Dante stayed determined

to reason out heaven and hell, Thoreau

fought through every opinion

for the altar of loving learning,

and Wittgenstein is a giant in philosophy

for he actually lived what he believed.

Next in the cycle is the tiger, who are known

as fearsome animals, and yet why do they live in the dark

forest? The tiger stalks the forest floor,

hidden by canopy, his paws sunk in mud,

hiding his vibrant stripes and powerful frame

from a world which much enjoys the pageantry

of power, would hunt him for his pelt

and the artifacts of his body. The tiger then knows

his power makes him weak, and takes refuge

in the humid jungle, fearing his mortality.

I find those born in the year of the tiger

shy, though when they feel welcome

they say whatever pleases them. Their awareness

of their weakness makes them magnanimous

to others, and yet it also makes them sulky.

A curious involution. Perhaps this is why Blake

146

asked, And what shoulder, & what art

could twist the sinews of thy heart?

I think the tiger knows that our frailty

is an inextricable part of the paint of the world.

Porter and Cortazar, Hölderlin and Dickinson

are tigers. Cortazar sought liberation

from convention, which is but a napkin,

and Hölderlin, nonpareil poet,

was the closest to divinity.

Next in the cycle is the rabbit, a creature

I honestly know and have seen little of,

I surmise, because they never leave their warren.

Rabbits can be thoughtless, dashing

beneath the tires of a car to evade

only to wind up dead. But I

don't mind them, nobody seems to mind them.

Those born in the year of the rabbit,

I have observed, differ from their animal counterpart.

It seems that those in whom quiet reigns

feel oppressed by their unintended tact

and desire the praise contingent on attention

or rather a riot interrupting their lives

for they never seem to care much for

the excellence of the thing itself. They're dreamy

and are off in their little world

happily nibbling the grasses on New England

lawns ever or running towards the tires of a car.

They feel the stings of that taciturnity

and seek outlets in which they are released

from the boredom that not so much surrounds
them as is self-imposed by their character.
Whitman, Wallace Stevens, Henry James,
and Melville, Robert Lax, so many great poets,
are rabbits. They seem to have acquired the fast
feet of the rabbit in their poetry. In Stevens
one sees play as transcendental,
and James' prose, its and's and which's,
are like roving landscapes of green.

Next in the cycle is the dragon, an animal
not real. Dragons seem to sense this,
embrace the contradiction, and yet are still
wounded by the fact. I am mystified by them.
They are made of the decentest stuff,
and yet they do not see people as human,
as in, full of emotion and sensitive.
I surmise, these are not absent in them,
rather they are slow in acknowledging their own
and thus slower in seeing them in others.
These same qualities mean they don't fear
sharing and extending a helping hand.
Those born in the year of the dragon
have their namesake's duality:
they can accomplish impossible feats,
and they can spend their lives slumbering
underneath gentle streams in contentment.
Sometimes they are so adrift
from their own feelings they find
a set of values completely alien –

and that is often not a bad thing.

Musil and Nietzche, Neruda and Kant

are dragons. Nietzche had the daring

to rediscover poetics in philosophy,

and Musil had the ambition to make sense

of a maddened world.

Next in the cycle is the snake, a creature

known for his wisdom – though sometimes

his luster comes from his scales, the brilliance

fools even himself, and this shine

of the snake is but a decoration.

Snakes slither through the mud on their bellies

not for love of filth but for caution

and for opportunity, as they like

the palpitations of the earth and

to approach their prey when they are least expected.

Those born in the year of the snake

are vengeful and yet precise,

are vain yet tightmouthed,

and so they are known for wisdom

not necessarily for their love of learning

but for their sense of how to deploy

whatever strands they know well,

whether it is at a dinner party or

in their abode nestling with their spouse,

this same sense necessary in a creature

who would long ago have been trampled

on the merciless jungle floor without it.

Joyce and Montaigne, Dostoevsky and Goethe

are snakes. Montaigne treated knowledge
as the best kind of ornament,
and Joyce desired every ornament known
to man – that is, he possessed every word
and every pattern words could comprise.

Next in the cycle is the horse, a skittish
creature, desiring to run headlong and
breathlessly down any green plain they see
though in every second of their joy they are
always fearing for their mortality.
Horses are straightforward in ambition,
yet complex in their emotions, too much, even,
and often their emotions are their obstacles –
though once the air is clear, and the corridor
is but empty space, they will reach their goals,
don't doubt it. One surmises they
set up their own obstacles sensing
their overfondness in running towards danger.
I myself find it strange that anything can be so
restless and so constrained,
but contradiction balances us all out.
Those born in the year of the horse
have no concept of dieting their hearts.
If you upset them, just like their sign,
they'll kick you in the chest – and it will sting.
Their sensitivity relates them to others and so
they possess a strong empathy – though sometimes
they are too forward-looking to notice.
These drifters do not mind a solitary sojourn

but something in their hearts has them yearn

for a partner to accompany them, someone

else's hoofprints on the loamy earth.

Beckett and Celine, Ballard and Barth

are horses. In Beckett we find

the irresistible pull inherent in words,

their power to wake up even the dead,

and though we could talk a storm on Celine

his running passages can teach indignation.

Next in the cycle is the sheep, a dreamy,

meandering, rather thoughtless creature,

who nevertheless dreams up the world.

Sometimes, they are in that world.

The sheep seems to find every luck and every

kind of person who will take care of him.

Perhaps they exude a kind of helplessness,

perhaps we find something appealing in their immobility

and a gentleness in their straightness.

Sometimes they chew and chew, sucking up

the vast horizon in the portals of their black eyes.

Those born in the year of the sheep,

in contrast, are quite thoughtful people.

They seem to love facts as much

as their sign loves grass, take much time

in ruminating on them, and interiorize them

such that they can find new things in old.

From their little world we find

they have acquired every eccentricity

carousing their fleece. They don't mind.

When a sheep has a notion in his head
it's very difficult to stop him, by reason
of his being constantly in a dreamy state.
Sometimes I prefer their dreams to this world.
Kafka and Swift, Twain and Proust
are sheep. Kafka is a cipher,
we think we know his world, we do not,
and we are not sure who is dreaming whom.
For Swift, I shall quote Yeats:
Imitate him if you dare,
world-besotted traveler; he
served human liberty.

Next in the cycle is the monkey, a creature
mankind owes running waters to.
The monkey would be master of all he surveys
if he were not constrained by his appetite.
He swings on vines, he smashes rock with bone,
he can learn language, and beg for food,
but he never seems to desire anything more
and indeed humans are struck by his arrogance,
or rather are uneasy with his facility
that they hunt him down and restrain
him and say condescending things about him.
But, admirably, the monkey says little
for all this and continues onward,
concerned only with the excellence of the task.
Those born in the year of the monkey
possess something of the animal's complex mind –
or only of the contradictions composing his being.

If he were to master this tension,

he might become all-powerful –

otherwise he becomes a sulky fellow

and is content sleeping naked beneath

the tree-top canopy, though other creatures

wish to climb up to him, admiring

the desires and tensions curiously absent

in them and seem to make him more.

Colette and Spinoza, Milton and de Sade

are monkeys. In Colette is pure

regarde, her senses suffice to master a world;

so mastered, she finds no use in taming it.

In Spinoza is the awesome use

of his rational powers to tame an indifferent world.

Next in the cycle is the rooster, a noisome

creature, but one whose luster and color

on their feathers cause us to forgive.

The rooster wakes the other animals at dawn

and struts his confines with a sure foot,

not because he is a busybody – though

a little too often it manifests this way –

but because he believes there is an order to things.

It's a shame he is so opinionated about it,

but, as it turns out, most fellows need a waking up.

And in the bright and wide sky he sees his kin,

the starling and the jay, twittering in the air,

and he sometimes thinks, If only I could join them,

oh these rude little wings of mine, and sometimes he thinks,

I flew once too, today I am biding my time.

They are sometimes unconscious of their vulnerabilities
and are then floored by them, and sometimes they
wear their weaknesses proudly, for they know
there is beauty in humanity, in fact a strength.
Those born in the year of the rooster
are themselves capricious yet right-minded,
they love ostentation, yet walk with a low head,
and they love admiration, for they see it as merit.
And although we dislike sometimes what they say,
no one stays asleep when the cock crows.
Faulkner, Gertrude Stein, Ford Madox Ford,
and Svevo are roosters. Stein finds
expression in order, pattern and repetition,
and Svevo sees beauty in our mortality.

Next in the cycle is the dog. This creature
will eat his own vomit. He picks the trash
off the ground, and tries to swallow it. He only
wants to play, and do no work. He leaves
his feces everywhere. He attracts every flea.
He is bred to be someone else's accessory.
His famed obedience and loyalty come from
being too stupid to set a course for himself.
Those born in the year of the dog possess
all of these traits. They're not known
for being particularly intelligent, and seem
to accomplish very little in their lives,
being content with a warm afternoon
and an unhurried saucer of milk by the door.
And they whine a lot. They're sensitive

to all. They fear everything at their doorstep,

see invisible enemies behind their walls.

I know all of this, for I was born in this year,

wish I could be born some other time.

Well, it is what it is. No helping it.

Gaddis and Broch, Voltaire and Virgil

are dogs. Well, Voltaire, he's a bit pompous –

but of what I have said, never mind for them.

Gaddis' prose proceeds in a trance

for the lives of the unjust are nightmares.

Broch is depressing, writes of an unfeeling

world because we cannot lose our humanity.

And though I make fun of Voltaire,

he is only reductive to remind us what is real.

It seems dogs write the most awful prose

so that their readers do not lose what is precious

like an overeager pup fetching the master's slippers.

It's a shame they don't write for the reasons

most do – for the sake of beauty.

I think they have no sense for it.

Ending the cycle is the pig. This creature

likes to lie in the mud all day, roll

in its filth, and fight for juicy

cobs of corn, and we find something

in this display something charming.

Those born in the year of the pig

share their namesake's simplicity,

their stubbornness, and their love for hoards,

and I don't mean wealth. Just like the rat,

155

he finds sentimental value in material,
and will fight to have as much as possible.
And yet there's something about this trait
that makes them dreamy, as if
he longs to arrange his life like one sure
square pigpen, where there is his water,
there are his oats, there is his bed.
The pig most of all wants comfort,
and we all like the pig for we want that too.
Rilke and Borges, Moore and Mann
are pigs. In Rilke is the deepest
yearning to be held by God,
in Borges is the innermost desire
to live in phenomenon itself.

And in this cycle, there are patterns.
Signs in sets of three share traits.
The rat, dragon and monkeys prefer control.
The ox, snake and rooster are vain.
The tiger, horse and dog are sensitive.
The rabbit, sheep and pig are dreamy,
though this dreaminess helps them find
other worlds beyond our sight.

Signs in sets of four share traits.
The rat, rabbit, horse and rooster
are anxious and proactive.
The ox, dragon, sheep and dog
are solitary and sullen.
The tiger, snake, monkey and pig

are charming yet defensive.

And signs can come in pairs as well,
themselves and their opposites.
Their opposites, like a mirror, contain
the traits most recognizable to themselves,
and yet the image seems unreal and
they can't get their hooks into them.

And beyond the lunar calendar one can also
analyze the movement of the stars.

Aries was the ram of golden fleece
who with Phrixus and his sister on his back
flew across the Dardanelles to Asia.
Helles fell, and so the strait is named
Hellespont, and Phrixus arrived to Colchis.
There the ram was sacrificed, and its pelt
is the same golden fleece accompanying kings.
Just like the ram, Aries is quick in action
and helpless in preserving their own life.
Their ruling planet is Mars,
named after the god of anal-retentiveness and discipline.
However, I associate the sign more with Pallas.
Dante associates the planet to arithmetic.
The tarot representation of the sign is the Emperor.
I can affirm I possess none of these traits
though I was born under this sign.

Taurus is the same bull of heaven sent down

to punish Gilgamesh for transgressing a god.
This same bull brought nothing but trouble
in its rampage slaying men and, finally,
even after taking its last breath, the loyal Enkidu.
And so Taurus comes thundering down in May,
bringing storms, welcomed showers for some,
and floods and battering winds for others.
There is something holy in Taurus's fury
whether it works for them or against them.
Their ruling planet is Venus,
named after the goddess of anger and harmony.
Dante associates the planet to rhetoric.
The tarot representative of the sign is the Hierophant,
and, indeed, these fellows are convincing.

Gemini describes the twins Castor
and Pollux, warriors whose chief devotion
was to the other, such that even death
could not separate the one from the other.
Two bodies in one, Gemini feels one way
then that, and every thought they feel
they feel strongly as if in agreement with another.
Conversely, they are slow in thinking
as if confiding with another person.
Their ruling planet is Mercury,
named after the god of deception and decision.
Dante associates the planet to dialectic.
The tarot representative of the sign is the Lovers,
depicting the movement of their hearts.

Cancer is the crab of the Lernaean swamp
who pinched Heracles on the foot by Juno's behalf.
The giant of a man then crushed it
and for its faithfulness in spite of its odds
the queenly goddess honored it.
Cancer seems to recall the mortality of its namesake
and puts on a naturally hard shell
protecting them during hard tasks
and keeping their emotions sequestered.
Their ruling planet is the moon –
yes, the moon is not a planet –
named after the goddess of wildness and illumination.
Dante associates the planet with grammar.
The tarot representative of the sign is the Chariot,
depicting victory regardless of cost.

Leo is the Nemean lion, the first step
of Heracles in his quest towards immortality,
who could not be defeated by mortal hands
and so the rugged man relied on himself.
Leo is the same, strong in disposition,
with their big heads being their undoing.
Their ruling planet is the sun –
which is really a star but whatever –
named after the god of relentlessness and indomitability.
Dante associates the planet with music.
The tarot representative of the sign is Strength,
depicting a maiden prying a lion's jaws open,
perhaps signifying that grace and strength coincide.

Virgo is Astraea, a goddess who once lived

among men and left them when she found

they would not abandon their dark ways.

Virgo is sensitive and likes to shame

others, perhaps because they shame themselves.

Their ruling planet is Mercury,

which they share with Gemini –

it appears these indifferent people

do not mind sharing the same abode.

The tarot representative of the sign is the Hermit,

for solitude coaxes wisdom.

Libra is the goddess Justitia,

introduced by the emperor Augustus,

the first and among the best of Roman kings.

Libra is even-minded and hearted

and yet sometimes dawdles when deciding,

perhaps to not admix justice and offence.

Their ruling planet is Venus,

sharing it with Taurus, for it seems

Libra relents to Taurus's passions.

The tarot representative of the sign is Justice,

depicting a judge with a sword.

Scorpio is the scorpion slaying

Orion, who through gritted teeth

swore to slay every animal on the earth.

As punishment the earth summoned the scorpion,

no warm-blooded, yawping thing he often hunted,

but a singleminded creature crawling in the dirt

160

that, by retort of its stinger,

reminds men they originate from the dark ground.

Scorpio too is silent and singleminded,

and sometimes simple in their affectations.

Their ruling planet is Pluto

named after the god of obscurity and wealth.

The tarot representative of the sign is Death,

which is in contradistinction to decay.

Sagittarius is Chiron, the mentor

of Achilles and Asclepius. Endowed

in archery and medicine, his equine

half represents lustiness, and his human

half represents restraint, such that

he saves his strength to pursue wisdom.

Their ruling planet is Jupiter

named after the god of capriciousness and steadiness.

Dante associates the planet with geometry.

The tarot representative of the sign is Temperance,

for this is the quality most useful to kings.

Capricorn is Amalthea, the milk giving

goat nursing the infant Jupiter.

The goat's disposition was as sweet as

the goat's countenance was ugly

and the lord of heaven purportedly used its pelt

to frighten the Titans in battle.

Capricorn's mind, potent, bears some of this crudity.

Their ruling planet is Saturn

named after the god of vindictiveness and deliberation.

Dante associates the planet with astronomy.
The tarot representative of the sign is the Devil,
depicting the sign's ease in their affairs
and their ultimate indebtedness to heaven.

Aquarius is Ganymede, a youth
Jupiter in the form of an eagle swooped
and took and in the awe of the heavens persuaded
the boy to be his wine-bearer,
teaching him the while the ways
of the heavens and how to rule rightly.
Aquarius is conceited, having been
favored by the heavens and naturally given
attention, and yet some among them
bear nobility and wisdom in endless store.
Their ruling planet is Uranus
named after the god of heavyhandedness and ingenuity.
The tarot representative of the sign is the Star,
for these fellows are never down for long.

Pisces is the shoal of fish aiding
Venus in various endeavors, at her birth
accompanying her to shore, and thereon
aiding her in escaping adversaries.
Pisces precedes revelation and birth
and roams toward people for curiosity,
and yet trusts their passions more than reason.
Their ruling planet is Neptune,
named after the god of surliness and pattern.
The tarot representative of the sign is the Moon,

as Pisces has the ability to illuminate.

Now, tarot readings, in comparison, are just bullshit.
But this entire analysis is also bullshit.

The analysis is a starting point to gauge
and react to the phenomenon of other people.
The intent is to realize that though we see
the same things and feel the same things,
we combine in different ways and in a
myriad of patterns such that thought shines differently.
Think of the analysis as a painting
which depicts nothing as it truly is
but the depiction itself is an invitation to consider
the different aspects of a landscape.
The system is an invitation to recognize
no one is the same as we are, and we must seek
in others their unique humanity, even when
they say things that are obscure to us,
and in pondering on their ways of thinking
we augment our own thinking, and our understanding
of how our own mind flows and of the world
that beteems with myriad meaning.

I am aware this knowledge will die with me,
these caprices, these obsessions, these fads,
and this is good, for life is one long caprice,
and when we mourn death, we shouldn't lament
what a man could have done in life, rather
the caprices and observations of life going with them.

And to me God is a pattern,

not a greyheaded, white bearded man,

directing the revolution of the heavens.

When the Bible was composed, its compilers

were careful to preserve the history and the

laws of the Israelites, as well as the

sermons of Christ and David's songs,

for these each describe a repetition,

a kind of rhythm, concerning the works of man,

and in this rhythm we see the song called justice

and in this rhythm we see the song called grace

and in this rhythm we see the song called truth

and these are all songs sung to the earth.

But nothing ensures these rhythms,

no one knows if the same note will repeat

or whether the song will be played on unto

the end of time. Perhaps the text

pierces through the veil to touch the mind

of man and reveals to us the mysteries

of this same mind, a tenant always,

living always so dark in us.

This rhythm, then, I call God

which we try to master with our reason,

and find our reason defeats our reason,

so we return to humble belief once again.

God is then eternal, God is all-powerful,

God is interminable, and God is good,

for we all possess God in our minds.

When we see the unjust hurt the weak,

God tells us revenge will be his.

When we see another man beg,

God tells us the goodness of giving.

When we feel the pains of our flaws,

God tells us to shoulder our burdens

and to believe in an impossible tomorrow.

By all reason, this silent speech

should be regarded as foolish and unfounded,

and yet we hold onto the pattern

sensing this lack of reason is wise.

And God speaks and sings to us,

cities shall crumble, the mighty

shall fall, and the earth set to decay,

and yet we shall all be here

after it all, in spite of sense.

There is no trouble

               if one calls God He or Her,

for in truth we are invoking ourselves

and the wisdom and fortune that led to our being,

the same we hope to glimmer through prayer

and guide us true through dark times

and nothing useless can come from speaking to ourselves.

And that is in part what art is:

an earnest conversation with ourselves,

and God is a kind of art, our expectation

of the outcomes of truth and justice

and is, moreover, the part of ourselves

reacting to injustice and fraud.

That song I sang to the demons, the seasons
and my footsteps had cultivated. In the perfumed
nights of spring, the muggy days of summer,
the bright evenings of autumn, and the wide
skies of winter, I passed through barren
fields, empty baseball diamonds, moldering underpasses,
walked by trickling rivers, lily pads floating on their forms,
listened to my feet crunch on the leaves of long trails
matriculating the song, for true song

                         concerns

itself with the earth and its people. We speak
of nations and cities, but there is only ever people
and their dispositions and their histories, and how
they combine to work and feed one another.
Our living animates this dead earth.

The song of the Germans is honesty toward God.
The song of the Italians is merriment with God.
The song of the French is reasoning with God.
The song of the Greeks is closeness with God.
The song of the Romans is warmth with God.
The song of the Latins is amazement with God.
The song of the Russians is solitude with God.
The song of the Chinese is harmony with God.
The song of the English is passion with God.
The best and deepest-seeking tragedies
in the English language, come from England.
And the song of the Americans? Well...

And perhaps we inherited Jonathan Edwards' hell

166

when we summon to ourselves visions of apocalypse,

whereas Mather held God was better served

by enumerating the Magnalia Christi.

Paine felt reason was lesser to Common Sense

and the Federalists, in their papers, resurrected the Republic.

Irving's van Winkle slept the revolution away, a

deadbeat dad, and down the mountain with hoary locks

complains with his daughter a twenty year absence.

And poor old Ichabod never seems to get ahead.

And the Salem trials, how long shall we prosecute them,

through Neal, Longfellow, Hawthorne, Jackson and Miller?

There is something irrational, illicit in the American consciousness

through these perpetually cackling, warty women.

And indeed there is something reflective, something of guilt

in the American consciousness, concerning our irreason,

as Fenimore Cooper and Longfellow keep writing of Natives.

And then Bryant and Dickinson write constantly of death.

The New Englanders find themselves very moody,

even outside Hallow's Eve! It must be the winters.

For Dimmesdale there would be no scarlet A's foregrounded

in sable had he at disposal a contraceptive.

And Ahab stumbles through a hundred thousand words

to be swatted by a whale's tail. Ishmael survives,

the character whose name had no relevancy those many words before

And Emerson sought a new religion, a new philosophy

on American soil, and stamped impatiently when it wouldn't sprout.

Thoreau, thankless admirer, wrote of Walden pond

and how much of the little he did there.

Nowadays everyone only has bad opinions of Stowe's titular hero.

Whitman conceives himself as both Adam and Eve

though he doesn't believe in covering himself in fig leaf.

And Twain wrote only of Quixotes, and his Falstaff is himself.

Crane's characters are always litigating courage.

Poe wrote a lot about murders, masques, the macabre.

The Jameses were two kinds of quacks: one

investigated phenomenonolgy, the other British table talk.

Upton Sinclair had a lot of beef throughout his life.

Stein preceded Joyce in experimenting with language

and would've been given credit if she weren't an accursed lesbian.

Ah well. We shall always have her description of roast beef:

In the inside there is sleeping, in the outside there is reddening,

in the morning there is meaning, in the evening there is feeling.

Eliot found inspiration from the most miserable of customs:

marriage. Porter too. She endured four.

Hemingway was a noble, rugged, worldly man

so the press profiled him. He seemed to dislike

Stevens, my patron saint of boredom

and wishful thinking, who much liked boats

setting sail on the banks of Key West, though he stayed

in wintry, snow-swirling Connecticut for some reason.

Faulkner writes always of Mississippian fuck-ups,

all burnt shadows etched from the Civil War.

Gaddis wrote a lot about fast-talking New Yorkers

who knew a lot about making money but nothing about happiness.

Fitzgerald was not Beautiful, but he was somewhat Damned.

Kerouac sought salvation on the road paved by losers and lowlives,

and Salinger's novels are beteeming with smoking sadsacks.

Cormac brought back the cowboy to slander him.

And here I shall mention Elison, lest he remain invisible,

and McPherson too, whose canvas was not blackness but sadness.

Barth asserts literature is exhausted, and then

writes thirteen very thick novels.

It's such a disappointment we can't claim Broch or Nabokov.

They weren't born on this soil. Sorry, I don't make the rules.

And then there's you, Bill, who wrote largely about

very sad, very bored, very whimsical Missourians

obsessed with systems imposed on them, those they

preferred to uphold rather than escape.

We curiously have no philosophy.

We do have a lot of essayists though.

It appears to me the Americans have one common theme:

failure. We put ourselves to the high measure of success

and distinction and fall horribly short. Our heroes

generally die. Many of them are alcoholics.

And we like to tell the audience they will go to hell

with no hope of escape and but a shrug of our shoulders.

And our obsession with Natives and blacks seems to point

to a guilt torwards our mortality we'll never clean.

Some make the Natives heroes, which is a bit

like Balzac writing of English tradesmen

or Shakespeare writing of French wine sellers.

It doesn't matter whether you are tall,

                                    or handsome,

or well-educated,

                or well-bred,

                        or wedded well,

or placed in a good profession,

                        or have polished manners,

or fought valiantly in battle,

                   or gave away charitably,

you will fail, if you are in the dimensions of this novel.

There is no D'Arcy proposing to Bennet, no

                   Wannop

proposing to Tietjens, no

                   Aeneas saving Anchises, no

Faust eluding the Devil, no

                   Dante expressing the ecstasy

of Empyrean, no

                   Pantagruel discussing finances, no

Kitty Scherbatsky wedding Levin, no

Oliveira conceiving the kibbutz of desire, no

Macduff solemn and duty-sworn at the death of his family,

a lot of American literature is despair

and very little contentment here and ever after.

It doesn't even make for good tragedy or philosophy.

Even the enemies of Dickens say, Blimey,

find we're far too sentimental for own good.

The Northeast certainly has a cynical style

of failing. Northerners are very absurd about it.

It likely comes from a cosmopolitan nature.

Writers are accused of pilfering from

the French, the Germans, the English, but

in truth we accept them but eye-rollingly

and find nothing serious in their teatime

analysis of social and political affairs,

170

though we take very seriously the crisis of the I.
In those countries, the characters participate
in crisis, for us, crisis is but context,
and disaster weaves with our being, but we
are not overwhelmed by disaster.
The South is very morose. The Civil War
will do that. The South has a deeper feel
for tragedy than the other states do.
That is how Faulkner came to be.
There is a passion and frenzy in their soil
encouraging the horror and the Gothic
to prosper. Their failure is not human,
it takes on a quality of inevitability.
I can't say much for the Midwest
nor the Pacific Northwest. The Midwest
is dusty going, from what I have read.
A lot of Rust Belt blues. A lot of
understatement. The Pacific Northwest
is very funny and sad, but I can't say.

Perhaps this is all a product of
our enormous sensitivity and moreover
our inborn sense of the tension between
all men being equal though not alike
and our knowing this tension needs
defending from the old world values,
values exercising hierarchy for the sake of efficiency.
We have a sense values, not just European,
have failed us, that they are birthed
from a soil soaked in the bloodshed at the behest

of an indifferent nobility and at the expense
of the humble. We can fail ourselves still
and so we keep to ourselves honesty,
honesty or the manifestation of hell,
perhaps the theme Edwards was invoking,
that if we fail to measure ourselves to our better
sense of ourselves, we will be punished
for our arrogance, by some tyrant or king.
In the trials given by Valley Forge
our troops fought not cannonade nor charge
but the biting cold and the hunger
the common people around the globe face.
At Gettysburg, where the cannon roared
and the rifles cracked, the soldiers received bullets
and the earth received their blood,
for she knows no bravery in assaults
and understands little the discipline in drills
and the dead are only so many bodies
that have sunk wordlessly into her abysses.
We did not fight cruel and insane battles
for ourselves to be more cruel – our empathy
for the weak and flawed, the solitary
and the constant, is our acknowledgement there is nobility
in living with our faults and attempting to overcome them,
regardless and in spite of ultimate failure.

And that is the character of America's song:
that of our humbleness toward God,
something we are loathe to give, proud
in our strength and our quick-thinking,

but we give it all the same, for God
transforms the humble into something beautiful.

And so the inscription on Lady Liberty's pedastal:
Keep, ancient lands, your storied pomp! cried she
with silent lips. Give me your tired, your poor,
your huddled masses yearning to breathe free,
the wretched refuse of your teeming shore.
Written by an Emmas Lazarus, whose namesake
is he whom Christ, from his vault of gifts, gave life
for neither copper coin nor token of Caesar's countenance.

And art is just that, our relation to God,
God whose name is not invoked, God whose attributes
are not described, God whose words are not repeated,
but whom we tell stories of in the mere act
of naming and arranging the things surrounding us.
When we begin life, we only have false words
in our mouths, or filthy words, whose meanings have
been dirtied by improper use, by myriad
associations, by references, by concepts
as they live in another person's blood, but not
in our own, and concepts half-chewed and reasoned too.
The singer first undertakes the process of cleaning
all words, discovering in them their multiplicity of meaning,
and they search through themself

                    beyond bias

beyond belief

          beyond public opinion

                  beyond

reason

      the essense of themself, to sing the words new,

as cleansed and colored through the sieve of their soul,

reflecting clear the numen of the world

as threaded through our own being, and in

this process discovering infatuation

with those who came prior and undergone

this same journey of self-discovery.

And this is my awkward tribute to you,

Whitman, you who found little among the leaves,

you who dared to call yourself a man

of the earth, you who sang of lifetimes

you have neither experienced nor met, you who

wrote boastings and affectations,

you with practically no sense for meter –

you who wrote

      Who is he that would become my follower?

Who would sign himself a candidate for my affections?

Walt, you are the one who set me free,

who permitted me to write bad poems, encouraged

me to write long sentences going nowhere

wearying all of the hearer's patience,

for you were the one who taught me writing can display

every jewel of art and still be useless,

if it lacks any shred of sincerity,

and in sincerity, in plain honest feeling,

in reason without cynicism, lies humanity.

Walt, you are a deplorable pervert,

but for you, I would like America to be

the final soil I rest on, if fate permits me.

Though it's no wise idea to tempt fate.

There is nothing pure about writing.

Some may say so, infected by Shakespeare.

We can no longer write Good hay,

sweet hay, hath no fellow, anymore.

For the Elizabethans wrote when writing was new,

and therefore all thought was new

and saw and invested new life in things.

Now thought has grown, and engendered

sitcoms, concert films, slide shows, high-

concept fantasy, documentaries, monographs.

There is no longer astonishment, no

O brave new world, that has such people in it!

Language to us is something cut up,

its pieces dispersed among hundreds of domains

and we are always borrowers and pilferers

of other people's language, and ignorant, too.

Everything, I admit, is new. We feel these machines,

these patterns and dances of gold-wrapped wire,

of circuits and electrical stores, comprising

a novel language, inscribed on green boards,

are distant from us, are circumstances we live through,

we don't live in them. Or language is a seed, sowed

across all the realms of human thought

and words of every shape and color blossom

vibrant in the ideas they convey and

proud in their genealogy, which is the

vine of human reason; and if we seek

to relate these words back to common language

then we look no further than their course.

When man beheld all that was in his sight,

what words were in his mouth? he made them all

painfully, unartfully, and yet surely,

for he needed someone to reciprocate what he saw

as he himself doubted the truth in his eyes,

a kind of long night without God.

And upon him, a miracle: he could say

there, on the grassy plain, a herd of horse run,

there a band of goats bray, and in the wide

sky, a flock of geese fly. And that is the word:

illumination that gowns the object and returns

their impression back to us, and when we

cultivate words rightly, they shine more

on the object, revealing more of their mysteries.

There is something of God in words.

There is something of the numinous

in words, some part of our brain

we are hardly able to describe.

Words are not big and heavy things

like bombs awaiting their dropping in conversation,

words proceed in a kind of martial dance

like the birds fleeing from telephone wire to wire

or darting among the arrowheads of the garden gate.

And in the former, you attribute them cowardice,

and in the latter they seem somewhat brave and deft.

"Fleeing" and "darting" are a kind of being

so to show you they are transformed in the moment

and will be free to be whomever after the sentence ends.

Words are a transforming. The objects depicted by words

never always are, for if they never changed,

sentences wouldn't proceed out of them. No object

is ever unchanged, even the dumb stone

which on every ray of sun, every breath of wind

argues to me its brownness, its hardness, its roundness,

and the past tense is unsure of what it is now,

and the present tense is but a snapshot in time,

and these tenses are awaiting the next sentence.

Words by nature express change, this is why words

are always in the process of changing, accumulating

new meaning, sometimes unrecognizable in the next paragraph.

Thus objects in their humbleness sing words

and we are but their receivers. And that is why

tyrants fear words, they especially fear

Is and Was and Had Been, for they perceive

these words, by existing, describe their works.

One only finds duplicitous or invented meanings in words

because they have not been silent enough among them.

Just as when we present ourselves to the glare of the sun

our eyes and linen are illuminated and behind us

a shadow falls, when we throw our glare at words

they share their meaning and their shadow

of the world in which that meaning does not exist.

The word is an arguer, and the argument shows

the very void it is arguing against.

This flying, this fluttering, dung-dropping,

mesh-pecking, chirping bird perched

on my windowsill, stays a while, then flies

to the distance where the sun holds the horizon near.

We consider him a paltry relation, for he is

small. But his opposing argument is not

a world without birds, it is a world without

flight, without flutters, without dung,

without peckings and chirpings, for all

he does is phenomena, are arguments presented

to the world. He is not merely a what,

he is also why and how, where and when.

Yes, even his shit is phenomenal, and implies

something in how we shit, and through this shit

we learn something about this material world.

The word does not imply its antonym.

The earth does not measure. It does not dictate

opposite. We do. The earth simply is.

The absence of beauty is not ugliness,

the absence of strength is not weakness.

Absence is a world where beauty and ugliness

are meaningless, and strength and weakness too.

We have no use for these words. They have no

meaning in this world. Thus the word,

when we receive it, argues to us

that things can be strong, things can be beautiful.

When we call a woman beautiful, we imply

she harbors an ugliness inside of her, she disguises.

When we call a man strong, we suspect

he has a weakness lurking in him. And so
when we call a woman ugly, we perceive
there is a beauty in her to uncover, and a man
we presume to be weak has a strength
he hasn't discovered or exercised yet.
And to call the dog or cat weak
is to use ourselves as a measurement –
that is, in describing their weakness, we use
our own as a frame of reference.
The flaws we accuse in others, we possess too.
If a man is sick, health was with him in some world.
If a man is dead, we see him alive in another.
For when a word is summoned, we see both
the meaning and the image of the meaning, as if
we were unlocking the door to the millions of
worlds in which things are and are not.

And now I propose to you an image
of a wrestler, a very large man, entering
the wide white room, stepping onto the
blue mat, brow pent and ready to face his foe.
Their hands touch, their limbs brush,
their bodies groan and their backs are bent,
and he bests his foe. He turns to the judges,
who then pronounce him strong. Yet what
they really mean is, he is stronger than his opponent.
Every word thus implies its comparative and superlative
and we get these mixed up. And there is another
meaning to the word not captured by these.
Bright to a man's face is a raging fire,

a sprayer of smoke, its fumes rising high

in the air, forming a kind of spiralling tower.

He hears someone cry behind the ash-covered windows.

Without intercession, they will die – but he too

will enter Pluto's house, of hellfire.

And yet he plunges into the inferno – and no one

can call him strong, for no one knows why

he judged it right to risk his own life.

And yet we have an inkling, though we may doubt,

that God pronounces him strong. Why?

Because, like Heracles, weeping for noble Alcestis

and dutiful to honored Admetus, he wrestled Death,

that void where words go and lose all meaning.

And that is the meaning of the word, considered

its absolute meaning, and closest to its origin.

Stronger and strongest are mortal, strong is immortal,

a word whose power can defy even our mortality.

And if this does not describe strength, worthless

is the word, for what else is worthy for its bestowal?

When we call a woman beautiful, we

marvel at her living, her moving, conversing

with her, and the way she apparels herself.

When we say of the dead, she was beautiful,

we mean she before us is almost deathless,

animated with the quality of life, so we believe.

When we call clothing or columns beautiful,

they are animated with their makers' minds,

for ideas possess more life than we do, and they spark

and course throughout our mortal creations.

And those who are fearless are not

eager to go to death. This is misconception.

Fearlessness is the complete absence of death

as a concept in the receiver's mind.

Fearlessness is not fetishization of death.

The truest of martyrs do not think death is honorable;

rather, they see it as merely moving to another state.

Therefore in every word is the shadow of sin.

Curiously, the words describing sin cast no

shadow of their better forms. Gluttony

does not imply temperance, lust does not imply

abstinence. And yet temperance and abstinence do.

I harken Plato: the good comprehends

itself and the bad, but the bad comprehends only itself.

Some words, therefore, are more powerful than others.

Some words by nature are only dark and cannot illuminate.

Or, these words are merely tools, ways to measure

the degree we doubt the veracity of true words.

Nevertheless, as I speak on them now, each possess unreality.

Regardless, the power of words comes from this tension

of their meaning and their absence of meaning.

A stone is not temperate, there is nothing for it to abstain,

except, perhaps, the sunshine sloping its back.

Temperance's power arises from the word's implication,

a world in which we are filled with horrible need

and the relentlessness that need inspires.

Strength imagines a world in which we are dull

and passive, unable to alter the events in our lives

to something more fitting to our disposition.

When we contemplate the meaning of a word, there
our better angels and devils are conjured on our shoulders,
arguing whether we affirm or doubt the word's meaning.
The devil shouts, There is no wisdom, there is nothing to know,
the angel attempts to soothe us, turn us toward
the truth, difficult as it is to know.
The devil rages, Mercy is made up by liver spotted fools
eager to defend their weakness, while the angel reminds
that we are weak ourselves, and humble in it.
The devil is a doubter, suspicious of the war
all words wage, and he prefers all the dark ones
because they're easy to achieve and overcome.
Thus virtue is a presence, not an absence
of vices, and this makes sense for virtue grows
in their listener, the more they collect the meanings
of words and are convinced of their truthfulness.
By no means is meaning absolute,
as much as the stars, long praised for
staying still in the sky, will last forever,
someday their torches will snuff and in their places
will only be the darkness their handshakes had been.
Every day brings new realities, new semblances,
every day we throw our gazes at things, shake from them
new truths, and so meaning must change,
not always to something true, but towards truth
for some unbeaten paths await the feet
that will discover in them their destination.

I use the Dao to perceive the meaning of Christ.
The Zhuangzi tells a story of a carpenter

and his apprentice, searching for wood, then appraising

a tree. The tree is a great big thing

the locals have worshipped as a god,

and the apprentice remarks how fine its wood must be.

The carpenter scoffs, and tells him the uselessness

of the wood, it's too brittle to make anything good,

and is surprised anyone can praise such an ugly thing.

Later that night he dreams of the tree,

which admonishes him. The only reason he

lived for so long comes precisely from his uselessness,

and that the locals worship him for his long-living.

In fact, he finds their admiration disheartening

for their admiration detracts from the usefulness

of his uselessness.

        In another anecdote, a criminal, named

Toeless Shushan, whose feet were mangled as punishment,

was admonished by Confucius, who told him

it was too late to receive instruction

seeing he had already been delivered just deserts.

To which the convict admonished, that the master

did not see the value of the spirit, which is always

whole, and could see only as far as his foot.

Confucius understood life and death were but

the same matter, and asked Shushan to stay,

though he would not.

        And so when Christ says:

And everyone that hath forsaken houses,

or brethren, or sisters, or father, or mother,

or wife, or children, or lands, for my name's sake,

shall receive an hundredfold, and shall inherit

everlasting life; how then do we interpret it?
It means, uselessness I shall redeem into usefulness;
the same shall be said for those who have sinned.

All of existence is as one, and we occupy
but one place under luminous heaven, and
tomorrow, another, and today were punished,
today you feel shame, today you want to curse,
but today is but a day in a rainfall of days,
so why collect the rain water of today
and hold it all account against life?
And Christ spoke in the Sermon of the Mount
to make amends with thy neighbor, to turn
the other cheek, to reject brother and mother,
and to worry not for food and water, for God
feeds and clothes the fowls of the air.
To follow Christ is but one position under heaven
and so why fret over one foot, and why
fret over all your worldly possessions,
for these are all merely positions too?

Tzu-Hsia asked the meaning of these lines:
"Her entrancing smile dimpling,
her beautiful eyes glancing,
patterns of color upon plain silk."
The colors are put in after the white,
the master answered, to which he asked,
Does the practice of the rites likewise come afterwards?
It is you, Shang, who have thrown light on the text
for me.

We are always in conversation
with the text, with the world. The texts are rivers
always flowing, or they are rays of light
warming the backs of their objects.
The words are neither Christ's nor Zhuangzi's,
they are ours, sung through our own mouths,
they are gifts, so we can see the truth,
they are free, thus they are equal,
and thus, when we quote these words
we are simply referring to ourselves
warming the meaning of the words with our breath.
It is we who must live, not the words,
it's ourselves who most need their warmth.

Well, shit. Why did I have to go and say that?
That's the problem with positive affirmations –
you must actually believe what you say.
I admit, I listen to neither, and only think
on the words of both after I masturbate.
Better to doubt everything, in this insane world.
You're less likely to be a hypocrite this way.

I can believe all I say, and yet the world
will make me eat my words one way or another.
The world knows every way to make a lie
out of the truth, or to distort it in some such way.

When the soul was dropped unto the earth
it was given form in flesh and mechanism of thought.
Indeed, the mind is mortal too. Just as the body

185

understands touch and smell and taste, the mind
recalls touch and smell and taste. What is immortal,
what is god-like in us is our ability to reason,
our power to see above these things and measure
them as befits us and our goals. This reason is perhaps
what people call the soul, wriggly word never leaving us.
That soul, given form, cried mightily
for it understood immediately it was alone
possessing only unique attributes as coordinate,
as color, as continuity, contour, emotion,
a lonely uniqueness that cannot be communicated.
This is the source of all man's pain.

Words, being expressions of mortal minds,
are mortal themselves. Only few are absolute.
All else have relative meaning, and thus describe
only scarcity. The word potato, for example,
describes on one hand the phenomenon of potatoes,
but its everyday meaning describes its presence
and possible absence, in terms of instances.
Articles – the, a, this, some, no – and determiners –
his, which, what – anchor the potato
specifically and temporally, that is, they direct
our eyes as to which potatoes we can manipulate.
I cannot think of a usage of the noun phrase
the potatoes implying only the concept of potato
meant to color an infinite green field
showered in inexhaustible potatoes
like manna found as frost on the ground.
Thus language orients our thoughts towards

scarcity and the actions toward scarcity.

Words that are more abstract and describe concepts

usually describe a state and not a category.

Wealth is a state; wealthy describes

a higher state than the speaker of the sentence,

or a state equal to the task of a given problem.

Nowadays the discourse on race

describes a going-up or descending-down of status

as history demonstrates time and time again.

Even if we look outside of society

the very idea of culture implies a presence

meant to detract or contrast from another race's.

The word human also has no absolute value

because everyone has in mind only the good ones.

Nirvana, recall, is a state to achieve,

for many visualize it as a promotion.

And the word blue too is described numerically,

a going-away from periwinkle and cornflower.

God is one of the few absolute words, signifying

inexhaustion. And yet inexhaustion is rooted

to a relative word – enough. Infinity too

has scarcity as a frame of reference,

for it means, number whose largeness

is not up for contention. Thus words reek

of corporeality, and worse, words excite

our envy by describing things and states

attainable or unattainable. We then curse God

for putting unattainable things before us

when in truth it's our language determining

the measurement of our abilities.

We were always relative creatures. We were always
like the wolf or the rabbit, we were always
obsessed with what was by our snouts, fallen on the
floor, we were always concerned with the sunset
because we were cold in our nakedness, we were always
precious with our preening, for it determined
our mating, we were always angry for space
for it meant less enemies, and we sought light
because we feared the dark. Hear me now, O Lord:
did you not know that light implies darkness?
Why give us the light, then, if it's ours
to skulk the darkness and cry ourselves softly to sleep?

We are solitary in our sadness.
We are powerless in sharing our world
nor are we able to affect another's.

I just don't know why I had to be born.

God, why did you put me on this earth?
Why am I not permitted to be as you
are, certain of meaning, knowing of what
to do next in this short life of mine?
Why when meaning gleams on my face
must I deny it and doubt it as if
it were some bastard I'm unable
to adulate out of some sick pride of mine?
What is the point of this awful need?

Or, are you, after all, the need,

are you the need to build and eat,

are you the desire to leave things ever after,

are you the question we are always asking,

and when we feel pain, we relate to you?

Are you, God, pain, and we

without our suffering cannot know you,

we, without our fears, do not perceive you,

it is not in feeling hurt we speak to you,

is it in saying, I have been grieved,

in our hearts, we reach out to you?

Well, what does that say about you, are you

a kind of nexus of agony, or are you the arches

through which we see beyond our pain

and so in saying the word inside of you

we transcend and see existence a little more clearly?

God is curiously the only word we know

that we barely understand. We can sit here and talk

about philosophy of justice and truth all day

but we agree by premise these are relative concepts.

A unicorn is but a horse with a horn on its head.

The word dinosaur has a definite meaning too:

at minimum they refer to the bones we found.

But God as a word defies all dimension and all

context. We could call the word, therefore, a lie,

yet the word lie too has a restrictive use

meaning that which is false under the glare of truth.

And a word must convey existence or

non-existence, and yet the word God describes neither.

God is a word outside of the dimension of reason,

but words themselves convey reason. Absurdity.
And yet, though we lash it with the slings of the absurd,
the word still lives on. It must point to some innermost
feeling in us, whether well-reasoned or not.
For that reason it is hardly possible to blaspheme God
as we can't conceive a dimension to do so.

Is God, then, not the wind on the boat's sails
nor the slope the water carries itself upon,
God is not every which way but
the hand and the eye leading ourselves
onto virgin shores? Must we our sense of the absolute
throw away, living in the tempest of our mortality?
For our bodies are balls of earth too,
and of quakes and gales we can betray ourselves yet.

We wrestle with God, as Jacob had the angel,
we come closer to God, as creator and perceiver
of all the universe, or as metaphor for truth
and justice, or even something so commonplace as
the fundamental mechanism by which our minds work.

And if one thinks they are so stupid
their questioning can only offend God
or they can gleam only wrongly or throw salvos
endlessly only to tire their own arm,
God stands upright and with strong chin grins
and laughs and says, I am so strong
and so wide, every arrow I can withstand, and every
stone thrown, you'll hit me with.

For he is the great question, not the narrow,

and when the day is down, the sun lowers

and the dusk veils the earth in murmuring light,

God takes every arrow fallen on the ground

and makes flowers of them, for, sentimental

fool he is, he thinks every question blessed

and every attempt at the mystery a truth.

Well, anyway, these are all nice thoughts

for we all know God is a huge fuck-up,

a failure of a deity, hardly a full man,

his knuckles raining hair, hair running

down his ankles, of a strain cruel and

intolerant and prone to fury,

always suspicious, always self-important,

isn't able to pick up his own clothes,

or put things on his shelf, or sleep early,

or comb his hair or iron his shirts,

God, in short, is a clumsy, sad, miserable,

unthinking and unknowing immature idiot, who cannot

make one thing love him, and we certainly hate him,

and when he does something so stupid

we merely clap our hands and say, Oh, God...

We're horrible, we're shit, we're violent,

hellbound creatures, we're inadvertent, clocks

set ticking towards the end of the universe, we're

pointless, we were born flawed, we weren't meant

to rule over this world, and question that same rule,

we weren't meant to have mind, and surely our species will

be phased out, when we use our atom bombs for

the right reasons, to end this long, tiring

experiment – we shouldn't have even lasted this long,

we shouldn't even be here, how many suicides

are we away before we realize

life was not meant to stare at death – the difficulty

of saying there is no question, is there being

no question itself is questionable,

for what even is the answer to a question we can't ask?

Shall we say, God is this question?

I can shape God now, and undo my traces next,

I can create God and uncreate him as he purported us,

and yet I never quite glimmer at his reality

in any of the bodies I mold and dissect.

God is something I believe in less and less every day,

find myself censuring myself for searching signs,

find myself hating myself for reading portents,

find myself cursing myself for being temperate,

and abstains from certain things, as if God

is watching and keeping credit in some account,

and I find myself questioning why I look for him in the

wind, in the earthquake, in the fire, in the

whispers of the sun at dawn, in the tears

on my face having survived another sleepless night,

I find myself chasing after him in every word

and every thought, and I hardly perceive him in the

Cogito ergo sum, and yet time after time, again and again,

I find myself speaking to him, if only to ask, why?

If I don't look, what else shall save me?

Myself? I have failed myself so completely,

I know little, as always, and I have done all

only to be here yet, screaming through all hell,

and shall I distinguish myself from these wan souls I walk among?

Voltaire had said, those who are in need of,

will always need God. Perhaps that is me,

perhaps I have disbelieved so long, distrusted

myself for so long and my own eyes, that I need

a God to tell myself to have faith in myself,

or at least some faith that there can be truth,

there can be mercy, and there can be justice,

and that there is some resolution to living,

and feeling, and sharing, and caring, and that

we *are*, that we don't understand, that there is chaos,

these are not sufficient in creating a world, and thus

we are not merely inventions, and we are left here

to only play long, elaborate games.

Let me, then, believe this most fantastic of premises.

Let me believe, for a breath, there is a pattern.

Let me believe, and see what awaits me at believing's end.

Let me believe, and when I'm done, I'll leave,

or I'll set my heart upon the pattern I do find.

And every shred of belief is useful in this age,

                              the Iron Age.

In ages past we were sufficient enough – we were once

light, and fed on every sunbeam, and felt complete

in the open air, and did not mind the dark

for we were bright enough. Then we were moonish

and fed on mist, we were flowing people,

always moving, never satisfied with one place

and so aged but never matured. We didn't need much

but to open our mouths and accept the moisture

in the air, and yet we felt, in spite of our sufficiency,

transitory, as if we had long departed a great river

from which we owed our beauty and origin.

Then we were ashen, and ate only dust,

the weathering and the decay of the world around us.

We were wayward and listless, carried away

in the winds, and sticky in the summer on trees and stones,

and as a result we came to believe in nothing

except on the changeability of existence and our fortunes.

This provender made us morose, then hateful,

for our lives depended so much on another's dying.

Men ate men, men shoved men, it was so easy

to do, we put our hands on everything and everyone

even though we couldn't hold onto them for long.

We then laid our snouts to the ground, and ate

dirt all day, we were indifferent to life

finally, and waited for the breeze to take us away.

And now we live in this age of iron, where all is

hard and cold, beauty and truth are separate

from us, and our nutrition requires us to eat

hard and cold things – we require another's life.

Though we can gleam the truth, for we do shine,

we are dim, and so all truth is dull

and stripped of all color. To console ourselves,
we build: all of life is stackable, smeltable,
malleable, and we believe we can build God,
hulking monstrous machine. Because we are malleable,
we make tools – we make words, numbers,
fires and hammers, all distant concepts from us
that themselves reveal no truth, they're only useful.
Most of all, we fashion tools out of ourselves:
some we call hunters, others are gatherers,
the bigger machines required farmers and smiths,
and the smiths of men we call instructors, rulers.
Sometimes a man's appearance is so warped
and he becomes so convoluted, no part of him
gleams truth anymore. His only truth
is in being part of the machine, his meaning
coming from the other tools using him.

There's no helping it. These are the cold and hard
days given unto men. The truth is not porous
like light, the truth is not gradual like water,
and as dry as ashen truths were, they still
came by the breeze. Truth here is labored on,
built slowly with syllogism and proposition.
There's no way around it. It's a shame our minds
can only work like the iron rings of a chain,
moving solely in the if-then. But this is how it is
with metal minds. There are perks, though.

Because thoughts are hard, they don't break easily.
Because thoughts are solid, we can share them.

Because thoughts are malleable, we can adjust them.
Because thoughts are a piece, we can get rid
of the ones we don't like, without moving the rest.
In short, thoughts can be transported and stored.
All men stand to benefit from a good thought.
It's how we've survived so long, we've stacked
our civilizations on improving ideas, themselves
not perfect or absolute in any sense, but better
than the last ones, so we stand a little more sure.

We all are spiraling towers with staircases,
stacked step by step, brick by brick, our spires
striking the sky, and our windows let in the stars,
we are lots of little assumptions, lots of observations,
lots of snap decisions under the siege of uncertainty,
and at the end of our lives, however small we are,
we die tall, at final breath, fall
into the piles we made ourselves out of.

We're towers, attempting to touch God,
and in this regard we are not all equally tall,
for we do not measure ourselves on the blank
space remaining to the wide blue sky, rather
we lay claim to the right to be tall itself.
The ballistae and bombs we shout from our towers
we hope destroy our enemies for we quiver
at the thought we are less complete in their completeness.

Logic itself is not truthful. It is structural.
It only guarantees traceability and repeatability.

Logic is unconcerned with the premises themselves,

it only desires scaffolding. A priori truths

are but little lies we tell ourselves hoping

the earth will honor them. Yes, hoping

is the key ingredient for conclusion. We hope

our minds remain constant, in spite of dementia, we hope

our senses are correct, in spite of darkness, we hope

we see a subject in its totality, or else

our incorrectness will inform our correctness –

and these hopes aren't even enough to feed the pigeons.

No, logic is a lot of bricks, carrying

us from premise to proposition to conclusion

such that every conclusion is precariously propped,

looks uneasily at its feet, sees, after many clouds, the faraway ground.

One of these days we will bring our trebuchets

and onagers against that great tower, the General

Theory of Relativity, that shining white, shimmering

tower, hitherto thought unassailable, hitherto

complete in its describing the physical world, hitherto

the envy of all minds other than Einstein's,

and we will launch our missiles and our rocks,

and the tower will deploy Greek fire and flechette,

and after many long, brave assaults, up goes

a column of dust, and that white ivory

tower will fall, so we can build more beautiful towers

on its soil, and even these towers will be flawed.

Every brick implies the dust it will become.

The soil our tower stands on implies

its sinking and slurrying into mud.

Every spade of mortar setting the tower

implies its own rusting and abandonment.

And because we live, we imply we die.

Our deaths are a tower too, one we build upon

every day, every hour. Mortality means

being contingent on another for our existence.

We are then's preceded by many if's.

We are ornaments. We are not necessary.

Why sing songs, then, and make more decorations?

Brow pent, pen in hand, even I,

in summer mornings, in spring twilight, in wintry

afternoons, doubt just why I write on,

when silence is more universal a language.

And yet, is silence somehow more immortal? neither

silence nor singing suffices, so what

shall we fill our hearts with?

A song, to me, is a search.

James, I am searching

for you, in the beaches before the Adriatic, down the

alleys of Trieste, where you wandered to your students,

through the marketplace, walking with Livia,

through the modern boulevard, of hazy lights, of

lawyer billboards, of dented traffic cones, of red

and green blinking lights, and crosswalks written in

chalk, of fried potato stands, of pot

shops, of bakeries, of halal carts, of Irish pubs,

James, where are you in all of this, what stones

198

did you step on, what clouds sailed over you, what songs
did the lady upstairs hum, as she strung her laundry up
to dry, James, you thought this life good for living,
so how did you deny its crushing you, how did you survive
its burdening you under its weight, its immensity
of detail, how did you see your right hand
in the volley of its arguments? James, how did you
live, for I desperately yearn to live too? And you,
Colette, and you, Rilke, you too, Gertrude,
and you too, Whitman – how does one live as an argument?

No answer. There's never an answer.
I'm always alone, without answers to my questioning.
They tell you, when you're young, immortality
lies in deathless prose, but even today
Homer goes slandered too. Shall I through these cold scripts
live in Dublin again, a Dublin James hadn't lived in?
You could only convince a child these scraps are real,
and even the song urging of me now, isn't real,
these are but the feelings of the moment,
and do I even know how I now feel?

We are just towers, we are but towers
built of foreign material, out of thoughts
we borrow from some other – we are oftentimes
another's invention, who among us is truly original?
Shall we pretend we are monuments in remote lands
hidden by rugged mountains and visisted only by deer
and our beauty is touched only by autumn rain?
And yet, what use is artifice in entire loneliness?

199

If we are brilliant, we distinctly feel borrowed,

and only when we are ignored are we novel,

so when do our eaves and cracks breathe out with contentment?

James, I wish this age would go away.

I wish to have been born before it

or after it, so I wouldn't have to see it.

Because we can neither see the truth nor

build ourselves true, we build elaborate lies,

soaring and penetrating through air, choking

every field, covering all green earth,

so vast it is, so elaborate our irises swirl,

that in our bewilderment, we call it truth

for we long to be astounded by that which we call truth.

How stupid, then, are we, to praise our contrivances?

And yet, I am still building. Shall I call it piety?

What, I am still building, word after word, line

after line, thought after thought, feeling

upon feeling, and the periods are bushy as

bees and the commas swarm like seahorses,

and I find, though I yearn for silence, I still

write verses, from top to down, writing

towers, still, for if I do not build

am I not implicating myself with dishonesty?

Are we not here to find out? Isn't there something

in the iamb and the trochee mirroring

the movement of our feet? or something in the noble

sonnet that so encloses our thoughts? of the gerund,

rivers are running, of the conjunction, images

conjoin, of alliteration, our hearts are refreshed

as if sighting posies, and of the metaphor, we find

all life is summarized in its single stroke of action?

Through the word we build ourselves anew every day,

we struggle with our words to find something true

in ourselves, we labor to build something if not true

then beautiful, not to call beautiful things gods

but to discover in the small the principles of the large.

Yes, this is why Socrates painted to Glaucon his Republic,

and, at dialogue's end, so master of his mind, he,

with one grand gesture, shattered this Republic,

its wise men and women, its happy ways and order,

and, magician he was, told his pupil magnanimously,

It does not matter if such a city exists,

for we have the pattern for ourselves to live by.

God had given our minds the analogy

so we may, by observing the action of that

which surrounds us, see the patterns of the eternal.

So Socrates said to Ion concerning artists, liars

are they, or the images and scenes sputtering

forth their mouths, are given them by the gods.

To reason with the earth, to tease

beauty from her scalp, is to ask upon scarcity;

you might as well shriek flowers out of seeds.

It's a shame we are towers, but truth

is something meant for ourselves, in our lonesome;

the truth is not for our neighbors nor for the earth,

the truth is what we speak within our souls.

How many hours did I sit mute, staring

at a long, blank piece of paper, pen set quietly

on its side, and only at the day's end, or the flicker

of a tree branch's shadow, did I write –

for what reason did I subject myself to this absurdity?

I hoped that, by putting order to the prose,

I would put a kind of order on myself,

that the virtues of the word would transfer to myself.

Shall I be so dishonest and say

in the very attempt, I did not believe in the act

itself? That we do, means we believe

in the result, on the mere magic of our having done,

and in the body of action, belief is real.

No wonder, amidst the world's surplus, we feel loneliness yet,

for all things know their shape and form, but ourselves,

and our souls, limitless, urging with waters, cry

out to know themselves finally in this veil of illusions.

It's no wonder I can't set these words raging.

It's no wonder I can't set these words to tears.

Words are a spiraling toward God, and therefore

cannot descend us into our sadness, only we may.

Words are steps by which we come to understanding

the truth of our mortality – and when the word

finds us suddenly cold, we cry, for we find

we never knew warmth until now, some other consciousness

considering and comprehending our mortality.

Hamartia: the fatal flaw the Greeks purported

to infect their hero, and cause his downfall,

but this flaw is but one spot on a field

of virtues, for the Greeks knew

the truth in tragedy is laid in our seeing

our humanity as light, in a dark world.

There is something gauche in the artist wanting

to inspire in their audience sadness, or fear,

or hate, or anger, or to provoke their listeners,

or, worse, to edify their listeners, confirm their beliefs,

these sentiments strike us as pointless and petty

for they appeal to our mortal wants, our desire

to face away our existence and to see only

up to our snouts, and we sense this arrogance

when the artist gloats before us, like a puppeteer.

It's joy that is brave,

willing to fight all,

it's joy that is worthy,

condescending to no one,

it's joy that is enlightening,

for it wears no clothing,

it's joy that is saving,

for, through it, we return to our being.

Joy implies misery, which manifests as

poverty, hunger, disease and neglect.

Because we naturally seek joy and the power

joy inspires in us, we find these words

utterly forgettable, we turn our faces to them,

and so ignore the poor, the famished, the ill.
These words remind us of our mortality,
and mortality implies immortality, meaning
suffering takes on the shade of inevitability.
Joyous words describe the state we seek.
They blind us because they are hard to attain
and because they demand in us
the actions to achieve them. These acts are called
giving. We struggle to give because we
are hard creatures, and reluctant to admit
we too are vulnerable. Giving will not
make a man less hungry, less sick,
or less hateful, but at least he knows he is loved.
And that is all the power despairing words have:
they incite in us depair, they make us fear
that if living is so harsh, dying is much worse.
Yet death is inevitable. It is merely
a new place. And so fear is unjustified.
And so, because meaning grows, if we allow
despair to grow in power, we allow men to die
in despair, we carry on us a curse ever
throughout our lives, that we will die
as these men did, and in dying, in living too.
What we then give is joy – though it is immaterial,
it's not enough to give a man bread
nor warmth nor shelter from the rain,
we must give kindness too, some shred
of our consciousness letting them know
they are cared by someone who doesn't even care
about themself. Without kindness, tomorrow does not improve

even with heaps of bread. We all must go to the grave –

that is the nature of our mortality –

but kindness is very close to divinity.

And not everyone is given to everyone,

sometimes it suffices to give to those we were born to,

however one can, in their capacity –

for we were placed in certain positions

in certain bodies, perhaps not for any reason

though we are given a choice to choose that reason.

James, "only we two may interchange,

each in the other what each has to give."

That is what I longed in my loneliness, to

exchange with another, to realize myself in another,

when I have lived far too selfishly to show

another just what it is I can give,

and consequently opened myself nothing to anyone.

James, I have apologized so much to you over the years,

you've suffered complaints, whines, rants

of mine, essays, preachings, rhetoric

on aesthetics, on politics, on society, human nature,

I should have realized, I was pleased to simply tell you,

and you were pleased to see I was pleased in saying.

We weren't made for silence, James, I know

that now, but neither were we made to know –

we were made to *say*, and to observe,

and to call ourselves true, and nothing else.

And that is all song is, it's singing

to ourselves, to realize in ourselves we are alive,
to put what we see and what we hear into words,
to make something solid of this always-fleeing –
we say to anchor our mortality onto the absolute,
for in a sense what is eternal is this moment
in this space in which it is ever a moment.
We write so we may live in the right now.

In the annals of literature there are no pure
rants, no tirades, there are laments
describing what was and is no longer,
there are complaints, sure, with their foregrounds,
there are harangues, which turn us toward
our better sides, and there are commands,
there are edicts, there are cruel speeches
that, even in their cruelty, paint better pictures.

Of the meanest writing, we have the satire,
whose words, by omitting what ought to be,
show in damning alarm what is not.
Of Swift, he found we were happier
in forsaking our humanity for marginal gains;
of Twain, we become even more barbaric
after giving the machine all our labors;
and Voltaire, I have developed a soft spot,
for he wrote "nothing could be so beautiful,
so smart, so brilliant, so well-drilled as two armies",
which proceeded to blast off the earth thousands of men,
not because you believed it, because these images inspired
so much indignation your only recourse was to laugh.

Voltaire, after so many American polemics, after
so many witch hunts, and threats and partisan shouting,
your laughter found in me some humanity.

God makes his residence in a joke.
Solemnity encourages piety, but revelation
lies in laughter. Revelation lies in the light
in the joker's eyes as he tells the joke, leaping
into his listeners' eyes as they await the punchline,
threading through the set-up, the joke's world,
and culminating in the punchline, throwing relief
not just on the world of the joke but
the joker and the listeners too as if through
the wordless word called laughter, what is understood
is some kind of truth, or something is exchanged,
something evanescent, yet real regardless,
even if the joke ultimately doesn't land
as is the case for Shaggy Dog jokes.

Unfortunately, I have no jokes for this song.
I'm not a funny person. At all. I'm known for being
so humorless that I once thought it would be funny
to teach a dog how to sing, Angel, specifically.
Doesn't make sense, right? What's the punchline?
But the song was a hit in the millenium's start,
and I didn't think the dog deserved any more treats
without my compensation, and so I labored over him.
When I showed him to others, I expected a laugh.
They should have laughed at me, for my effort.
Instead, they thought the dog was quite good.

This dog sings better than most singers on the radio,

they said. You should put him in competitions.

I had lost a bit of my allowance on treats,

so I agreed. He won these competitions,

the judges loved him, they shook his paw,

and he moved ever to greater national

dog singing competitions. I presented him

to a competition in D.C., the nation's greatest

dog singing competition. I was nervous,

he was nervous, he wanted to bow out,

but he seemed to do well, the crowd liked him,

the judges swayed their heads. When they gave

their scores, one gentleman presented himself

to the mic and said,

This dog is not Shaggy.

You know, I used to be funny once. I once

used to like jokes, liked to hear them, liked to

tell them, and liked to be funny, see smiles

on people's face. I'm not sure where that went.

My mother had told me stories

that my father worked two jobs once.

One of them was to clip tags onto

T-shirts as they came down the conveyer belt.

During Mao's time, education was seen

as bourgeois and so was privileged to

peasants who themselves couldn't afford it.

My father lived in the city, and so this privilege

couldn't go to him. Thus he had little educaton.

208

And yet he ensured his children's
and I believe he has a degree of his own
though I assume he hardly uses it.
But it's nice to have some artifact
saying you accomplished something, paper
piece it is.
            I always wished I could be
in accord with his lifestyle. I wish
I did something in my life signifying,
I made something of myself, because
of you. I wish I could've given him
a better son. Instead I find in him
folly. If I have any belief in diligence
and commitment, it comes from him.

When I was a kid, he would take me to the library
watched as I snooped through their spines, picked
out books, Magic Treehouse, Harry Potter,
Animorphs, Captain Underpants, Eragon.
He himself never read. I don't know why
he endured the trip. I don't remember
any of the words in those books, but they
led me to aspire to the classics, a journey
leading to you, Bill. If he hadn't taken me,
perhaps we would have avoided this misfortune.
Don Quixote, Catch-22, A Connecticut
Yankee in King Arthur's Court, I read
a lot of books I neither liked nor remembered
at the tender age of, I think, fourteen.
I don't know why, I don't know why so

much of my life had to be this way. The mind

of a teenager is like a god, but I peer through

in hopes of finding just what my destiny is.

Perhaps I did it out of distinction. Perhaps

I operated on some value system imposed

by my parents. Perhaps I fooled myself

into thinking the books possessed power

despite not remembering a single damn thing in them.

Perhaps it's the Chinese way of thinking

that society is ordered and therefore sorts

the good and the bad, and I was apportioning myself

to the good by doing what revered men did.

Perhaps my father believed in that thinking too.

Yet in my warped way of thinking I thought

I uncovered a hidden pathway to fame

and that in becoming a novelist I could attain

a kind of isolated success from

chemistry and physics, the path all others tread.

Perhaps I felt completely mediocre

in a system that didn't reward me

and so created my own, to laugh at

everyone else while I moved slowly to riches.

Perhaps I felt finally divided

from my friends and peers, didn't relate

to their ambitions or lack thereof.

Perhaps I felt finally divided

from myself, and the senses my body grew towards –

perhaps my sense of self grew slower

than my sense of who I could be,

and I felt frustrated by my surroundings, for they

did not honor me with what I desired.

Perhaps in the loneliness of my soul

I raged that no one could reach me

and so raised up even more thorns

to make this all the more true.

I never liked New York City. I never liked

its carved streets, its periodic lights,

the parade of its shoes, the release of its cars,

its ghost, behind the frosty window panes

of tall buildings, the facelessness

of its facades, and the ceaselessness of its

commerce, as if the Moirai draw fates

wherein each and all born are bored, behind counters.

I disliked how preplanned, predetermined the city was,

unable to find in itself spontaneity.

I never liked being poor. I never liked

Bagel Bites, Hot Pockets, TV dinners,

packaged ramen, frozen knishes,

Entenmann's, Kentucky Fried Chicken,

while my schoolmates talked about golfing

and long trips out of the country.

And the poor are not humble – they dream

always novel ways to spend money,

for that is their sole aspiration.

I never liked being a man. I never liked

the blood boiling for sports

or the constant crowing for bloodshed

or the innate desire to seem superior

so often foundational in boys, and I disliked

211

how boys were supposed to approach girls,
as all-balls, as blood-filled, as calling
girls "baby", "honey", "sweetie", as holding
a girl's hand, to imply she is yours,
as leading a girl's mind, as drawing her
to water, as seeing her as something to wine
and dine, for all they only care about is cash,
and I resented all of these aspects for when I
tried my hand at them, I failed utterly,
and decided to forsake them, ever and ever,
and yet at night my flesh rises and I
can't deny the way my body was made.
I never liked being Chinese. I never liked
we were good at math, I never liked
we had slanted eyes, and yellow skin,
I never liked we had tiny dicks, I never liked
our being square, I never liked we were
destined to white-collared shirts and glasses
for ever and ever to the end of our lives,
and I never liked my forebears, faceless
drones meant to populate city streets.
I never liked America. I never liked
this braggadocious, boisterous, plain stupid
country that only knows how to lie
such that lying is the means to eat bread.
I always hated its arrogant, reckless,
law-unabiding, law-inventing people
who seemed never to have any courtesy
or contentment for being alive.
And I hated all of these things so much

because I have tried to make peace with them
and they rejected and spat on me for my pains.

I never liked myself. I wish
I had been born anything else, or someone
else could have been born in my body,
because I was never able to make any use
of my fate. Sometimes it seems the way
to correct these cursed circumstances
is to cancel myself from existence.

That's how it is: we're cursed by
our mortality. Stress and genetics are
curses. My grandmother has dementia.
My grandfather smoked mighty, and got
lung cancer. And they had to put a catheter
into my father. First time he cried, my mother said.
That's my fate, too, to be broken.

To be broken by illness, to be broken
by the need for money, to be broken
by children, to be broken by
an unloving wife, to be broken by
the complete meaninglessness of moving on
and the envy that comes from another's contentment.

And in so doing, I become my parents
and end another cycle in a long history
of humanity going through the same painful
track it has plod along since its inception.

Is it arrogant to conceive something else?
Is it churlish to want something else?
Is it precocious to even think on the question?
That of our being dull elements in history?

And how can we call anything love in a mortal world?
How can we call something love, when time will dust it over,
when space will dilute it, when color will make another
girl so appealing, in her own way – it's not
that everyone born on this earth is not special, it's more
we are too special, we can't comprehend our uniqueness,
and so are paralyzed in deciding one thing
and so become commodity, merely attributes
to advertise and to sell to whomever wants it.

Thoreau gave up his various professions.
Broch gave up his textile factory.
Whitman gave up writing, for nursing.
And Hölderlin gave up everything
to write the words his contemporaries declined
which would crown him immortal and best of poets.
And here I hesitate, unable to commit
to the words my heart in earnest has said,
because I fear the meaninglessness of this mortality.

If I were born out of New York, I wouldn't be lumped
with these overly-clever Manhattanites.
If I were born a little more wealthy, I'd feel at ease
quitting my profession and taking up a writer's post.
If I were born a woman, I would explore

the literary possibilities left behind by Colette
and Gertrude, their sensuality above sensuality.
If I were born white, my writing
would be accepted, however weird it is.
If I were born black, I'd continue
the legacy of the Harlem Renaissance.
If I were born Hispanic, I'd innovate
on the ideas of Cortazar and Borges.
If I were born anything but Chinese,
I wouldn't be confined to writing
fucking immigrant literature all life.
And if I were born out of America,
I might live with people who love art
earnestly, plentifully, ardently.

Son.

Of.

A.

Bitch.

Did God give us self-introspection so as to
encourage us to empathize with our fellow humans? Or
did he allow us to reflect on our bodies to inspire
us into conflict with the other, to affect madness
onto those who can conceive every world in which
they are happy, any that is not this one?
Because we were not meant to think so much – yet
the world constantly reminds us of our poorest attributes.

What I desire

is a kind of purity

of flavor, of sensation, of pleasure,

of joy, of ambition, of heart,

a kind of, simplicity and completeness of taste,

a unity of taste, if you will,

unifying all the parts of the body

and soul into the experience, such that

the flavor of one does not impinge another,

my sight in its joy does not disagree

with my touch, and in my ears is all music,

I suppose, a true transcendence,

a pure merging into the world's whatness.

And yet this ease, this completeness

of being, I am thinking, is impossible,

for the appetizer suggests on the main dish,

the song is interrupted by the construction crew,

or mother enters the room while we climax.

Pure was the tapestry we were cut from

and when we long for pure joy we are clutching

that piece of cloth, torn, we had since birth.

The only thing necessary to existence

is existence. It's so difficult to believe.

This is how essential existence is, and yet

how meaningless as well. We are just *here*,

and notions of good and bad are relative. Can this

even possibly be true, or are we so attached

to our mortal senses and mortal reason we cannot

even imagine a completely independent existence?

Do we sense this quest for essentialism is unnecessary,

merely a useful exercise? or is it more correct

to think, when the soul was given mortal form,

it sufficed to *be*? that it was cut

as if from a tapestry of infinite pattern,

a riff, a moire, a blend of color, and given mortality

is meant to merely color the existence we call

this world? is it then we quest for purpose only

because this earth has a concept of time,

and so we believe in duration when, in truth,

we always are, these attributes of ours are colors,

and, looked at cosmically, we are simply meant to be beautiful,

which, by existing, we already are?

The truth is, all of these are true.

We simply cannot know, limited our language

and our beings are. It suffices to say,

we are here for no reason other than to occupy spacetime,

we are here to live however we want, for all life

is ornament and our purpose is to merely observe,

we are here to create measures of good and bad,

and this exercise is fruitless as no measure comes of it,

and these three very different meanings are all

equally true, and the truth lies not in choosing one

but in accepting all of them and making whatever you will

out of them. And this truth strikes us as cute,

because there is nothing more to it – but the truth is,

there is, in fact, nothing more to living.

The Xinhai Revolution led to the republic

and, for a time, China had some peace.
And yet something of the emperors
stuck around in the prevailing attitude,
and Yuan Shikai tried to take the reins
with the Hongxian Monarchy. He failed,
but the damage had been done; and when he died,
powerful warlords sprung up all over
growing like fennel in spring
whose language was Gimme, who acted
like wolves. Slaughter won the day.
Chiang Kai-shek would reunify the country
in land only; he had no sway over men's
spirits, and the conquered continued their ways.
In this era of lawlessness, of the strong
stealing from the weak, the Japanese invaded
in the guise of the saviors of Asia,
and in the bloodbath my grandparents were born.
It is said they dwelled in the dark forests
and stripped the bark of trees to eat
because they feared the invaders' bayonets.
Nothing separates us from animals,
though we think otherwise. In this
swirling dust cloud of a world, we take
every form, good or bad.
In a world where men are brutes, squabbling
over the thin roots in the ground, I don't know
why my grandparents wanted to live. But they did,
and I'm here because of them.

And now, they are dead. I with my fingers

218

try to touch them like a phantom limb
and ask, what did they live for, and what
did they accomplish, through me?

Ah, Chinese to the bitter end, I see. Ancestral
worship works strongly in me. And yet, if we
the living say, death has no meaning
and life neither, then can't we the living add,
but we, through our living, can give it meaning?

Is this, in a sense, the elixir
of immortality emperors sought?
That the baton-passes and handshakes we give
transfer us as pure will, down the avenue of centuries?

I sang of peasants and emperors in my song
of folly, but there is another class yet:
that of the scholars who obeyed their ruler
with their knowledge of the world and of men.
Not all were selfless, not all were honest,
but all were smart, and they believed
the Son of Heaven would recognize them.
But he is no god, and sent many of them
to the frontiers. Some of them incensed
him, for the mere fact of their living,
and he punished them, as the Qin Emperor
punished Sima Qian, castrating him.
And yet the Grand Historian lived on, to finish
the history of the country so all men
would know how their ancestors lived, and so

to finish the work his father began.
Endless good men have been punished
by fool rulers – the Chinese have only
themselves to blame, for putting themselves
under the yoke – and yet Du Fu, Cao
Xueqin, Qu Yuan, and even Confucius
lived on to sow their wisdom to the ages
and to let their descendants know they, too,
lived, because we are always forgetting
just how much life radiates in us.
And, this is the life led also by
Whitman, Dickinson, and Thoreau.

In some other world there is some other
me, living as a recluse in the barbaric
wilds, watchful for the cock's crow at
dawn, observing how the pears hang heavy
on the boughs, quietening my breath
to hear the river, remote, murmur, and towards
the mountains I throw my gaze at the
magpies and the distant cranes, then walking
to my pen of pigs, to feed them the day,
humming songs of yore happily under my breath,
unconcerned with poetry, for this all is poetry.

I try to divine beauty

                    through a good recipe.

I try with my mouth to understand

                    the earthiness

of the lentils, the leafiness of spinach, the sourness

of olives, the tenderness of a potato, the crispness

of an onion, and the chewiness of a tomato,

I cut the tomato as pages, I dice the carrots

into cubes, and the peas tumble into a bowl,

as the pan sizzles I press my spoon

onto the tomato, bleeding it of its juices,

leaking into the pan where it blesses the

onions and carrots and celery with its sharpness

and marries with thyme and rosemary

enveloped in a shaky cloud of steam, lending

the kitchen its smell, or the sprays

of turmeric and coriander and cumin, lain on

ghee and warmed chicken broth, or rice fried

with butter and heaped with mushrooms,

olive-colored skin and black gills,

or a length of chicken breast cut into crescents

lowered, with salt and pepper, into a cup of soup,

or kombu and bonito making a clear broth,

clear as the eye espying it, clear as the soul drinking it,

sometimes clouded with a clump of miso.

I try with my eye to understand

                              Rothko's hazy fields

of black, Frankenthaler's cloud of color, Jacquette's

tendrils, Rodin's exultations, Millet's

pious animals, van Gogh's lushnesses, Ruysch's

elaborate flowers, and Gongshou's lonely hermits.

I try with my ear to understand

                          Ayler's

fiery saxophone, Joni's murmuring guitar,

Iggy's lascivious Lord!, Blind Willie's hums,

Merzbow's squalls, Neil Tennant's Take
my hand, and Ka's I hope it's borrowed time
when my time comes, for my time wasn't kind.
I try to understand

      with my mind

           how the d's flash

in understand and mind, how the t's and d's
of try and understand are like a dancing, ending
with those d's, as if ballerinas on their tiptoes,
how then the i's in with and mind dart
after the reed-like t's and d's, as if rushing
out of the woods of understanding and into the shimmering
mind, and how the t's are thin like
stalks of clovers, but d's are deep, like tubers,
and i, the tittle detached, is like illumination,
yes, the tittle the mind separate from the body
so that i belongs so well to light and fire,
and the i in light raises the tongue to the roof
and yet the underground-dwelling g lowers it down
as if in your mind the light, after flaring up,
is already dimming, and yet the f in fire
makes the lips mince, dancing just like the flickering
flame, and so too does the terminating re
raises the tongue up like the fire's tongue.
And if we are so blessed with color and shape
we're just as blessed by the words for flowers,
like the mountainous hyacinth, the pretty
peony, the whimsical daffodil, with two f's,
bluebells soothe us with three slender l's,
the honeysuckle invites light in with low u's,

222

and carnations are steady with anchored n's.
And isn't the rose a little like its creator,
layer upon layer of warm color? or is
the rose color growing out of color? is the rose
like Empyrean itself, not growing tall or wide,
but folded unto itself, throwing upon itself shadow?
or did men so love roses, we made them
or allowed them to be this way? is the rose instead
what a man's mind is, a spiraling staircase,
or do we say, rose, we aspire to you?

When I was young, beauty to me was
a beautiful girl tossing in bed,
the linen aroused by her moving,
her skin aroused by the touch of my hand.
Then, as I grew older, beauty was
Times Square's display of fireworks,
the Dragon Boat Festival, jets soaring
through the air, abracadabra,
aliens beseiging New York, and the hero,
against all odds, triumphing over the villain,
pomp and circumstance, spectacle, essentially.
Then as I grew older, beauty was
James singing of Gerty MacDowell
surveying Sandymount shore, Ford describing
the Germans' artillery like a giant boxing
the mountain, a thing out of Goya,
the dwarves and imps of the Consul's Mexico,
Goethe's Classical Walpurgisnacht,
Tennyson's odes to the purity of

Arthur's knights, Colette's adventures
with green sealing wax, and Rilke's
anemone waking up to the morning.
And now that I am old, beauty is
Beethoven's one hundred and thirty first opus,
the storm of Coltrane's Ascension,
Hölderlin's dithyrambs, and Stevens'
lonely, melancholy, empirical poetry,
for I live finally in the abstract,
my house is finally thunder and squiggling
saxophones, lines only, broken.

We frequently take joy as an overwhelming,
we frequently think joy is entire,
as if our bodies feel more joy than our minds,
or, rather, we are so disgusted with our minds
and their limitations, we wish them no joy.
Joy thus is an explosion, a burst
brief, something indisputable, inevitable
even, and after it is gone we are left
to remember joy, as if squeezing joy's hand
lasciviously, though she no longer answers me.

I have only felt this kind of joy once.
Every other time, something got in the way,
an appointment, an alarm clock, a hungry
belly, unwanted attention, anticipation,
and yet when I saw the Marriage of Figaro
and I heard the duet between Susanna and the Count
beginning with Crudel! Perche finora... the Count

lamenting Susanna won't return his affections,

something overcame me in the dark hall,

something warm, white and bright, something swelling

in my chest and throbbing behind my eyes,

in the unusually harsh winter of the city,

where that day long I endured biting rains,

as the Count, his affections returned, sang

Mi sento, dal contento!... expressing how his heart

was leaping in joy, I felt light

and I think I died, yet, I thought,

it's okay to die now, for I am in heaven,

as Susanna and the Count interchanged,

as Susanna and the Count contrasted,

their bodies and their words weaving through the stage,

as the strings soared, as the woodwinds

made breezes wrapping the hall in spring,

the Count's baritone shaking with gioia,

and for a few brief moments I was happy to be here

before I descended and entered the mortal realm again

tired and awaiting the Deh, Vieni,

where Susanna longs to crown her love with roses.

Ah, another moment of deathless beauty,

when I saw one of Monet's views of the Epte.

Are there trees more beloved in all of art?

Those four, standing above the Epte's waters,

the river reflecting all of their values,

the leaves of the tree reflecting the dusk,

the bark of the trees inflamed by the light

such that Monet is praising the trees'

steadfastness in the swirling color,

yes, I died here too, I had tears weigh

my eyelids, I felt close to God,

for beauty lies in the light thrown

on the trees, creating emeralds and pinks

and pearls and blues from the sky,

in the trees throwing their images on the

Epte, such that they were ghost-like, ethereal,

living their second life on the water's mirror.

Life, to Monet, was like a rain,

and at no point is one part of the rain

most rain-like, its droplets tumbling

through space, striking past the lantern

light, bursting onto the pavement as white cups,

and then to surge on the asphalt in rivulets,

bestowing white foam on the greedy gutters.

Is there a point to enjoying the pigeon,

the starling, the chickadee, occasional robin

and blue jay on the branches of my window,

do I see myself in them, do they carry

the raiments of the world to my viewing,

are they are reminding me, after longest night,

that the world has variety in it still?

Why can I watch the cat sleep so long,

so still, and yet shaking, his eyes closed,

his paws crooked, his mouth in a bow,

back supine on my Sleepwalkers,

is it that, even in resting, he is alive,

that even in sleep life is executed,

that inactivity even is phenomenal,

and is that what we all are, loved

by God, even when we are sleeping,

indeed spend all our lives walking unawake?

Beauty never is. It lies in action.

It is a becoming. It does not come after,

it is not built up, nor does it climax when

Susanna sings the last ti' vo' la fronte

nor the first. Like Aristotle's sleeping hero,

beauty is within all of us, awaiting the time we do.

Beauty is the exchange of the world

flooding our eyes, our minds comprehending its

attributes, and the revelation possessing us

where we depart for a moment from antient castles

and sees ourselves new and entire.

The mind perceiving beauty is not beautiful,

nor is the thing inspiring beauty beautiful,

that the one allows the other to participate in beauty,

that is beauty, the warm hand

and the eye in confidence, that you are

trusted, and you are given grace.

"Only we two may interchange,

each in the other what each has to give."

And I see now that is what the metaphor –

no, what all of fiction – works within

us, an interchange of our worlds,

of two things unknown to the other,

two moons dancing in frigid orbit,

in their impossible loneliness lending

the other their qualities, transforming

them in the brief and hopeful moment,

and so doing realizing in them qualities

they hitherto were unaware of in themselves,

for when I say, her hair is like rain,

her hair is falling on the side of her face

throwing light in her eyes, swaying

in the wind, and the rain too

has something like the amber color of

her hair, and I love them both

and my heart feels susceptible to both.

Nothing in the metaphor, analogy, parable,

simile, allusion, image are true,

but their action of relation is true

for all of life is sung out of pattern,

pattern of pattern, fustian threads winding

over and below the other, and all of life is one,

yes, all of life is one, they come from one mind,

our mind which brings the world into harmony.

Yes, that must be what I want, interchange

with another, not an adoration

of another, not an honesty with another,

not a transaction with another, I yearn

to incorporate another into mine, friend,

lover, partner, I want to transform,

I want another to transform, by my hold,

by my glance, by my kiss, I want to be complete

in another person and be united in them

to know something good has finally

left me, to know there are good things

in me, and I want to find in another the good

in them, to know the world too is good.

No wonder I longed afer books, for there

I found the minds that so loved

the world and loved too those that came

after they put their love in words,

and then there is the love protecting

those words over the callousness of time.

Books are products, then, of love

and I loved interchanging with them

our hopes, our anxieties, our joys.

A book, poem, a letter is holding

the writer close to the reader.

I long to interchange with your

auburn hair, I long to interchange

with your dark eyes, I long to

interchange with your pale lips,

for in interchanging with you, I relate

to God, for you, to me, are God,

and your and my worlds are intertwining

and your and my worlds are revolving

and I feel comforted, in your powerful gaze.

Yes, that must be what I desired, all

this time, in my rage, in my follies,

all the protectiveness I felt towards others

and the desperation I saw in myself,

I longed to be seen by another as if

I were new, believing I could be new,

believing I could satisfy another's eye,

for isn't that why we go out into the world

and attempt to find joy in the world? to see

the things reflected in our eyes, filling

our minds, and so doing, finding something in

ourselves in this contemplation? Aren't we searching

for something in ourselves through the things we cherish

as if we lived with them in another world,

as if we loved them before, they speak of our eternity?

And perhaps this is all sin is,

missed opportunities to relate to another's beauty,

to see it truly and purely, to deny it from ourselves,

and knowing we lost one pathway to connection

we know in some way we have damned ourselves.

And I haven't recalled, when I was young

I used to write fanfiction on internet forums.

it seems, somehow, I always was.

And perhaps it was after when for acclaim

I exclusively wrote, but as a child,

I think, for the past is a place enshrouded

in fog, I wrote for play, to grasp

at a world whose passions and dialogue

were delightful to me, were colors to put

not on myself, but to thrill the page they're on.

I remember a young woman was struck

by a phrase I wrote, about a cat:

My brothers and sisters were scattered, like stars.
I myself thought little of it. There is something Rilkean
in how we regard our own words, that we
are unaware of our ultimate character. I don't quite
understand how these words can strike anyone,
but I am struck that someone else can be struck.

In those days, I wrote prose
badly. These days I write songs
thinking I'll be forgiven them again.
But in those days I wrote prose,
only one of my trifles was read.
For reasons I still don't understand, he
hhen showed the work with his mother,
who evidently gave it polite praise.
This is a mysterious exchange to me
because I don't understand why I was so touched,
whether someone found excellence in it
and thus found excellence in me, whether
someone shared in my emotions, and I felt
seen, whether I was gratified something in me
was real, it was now part of someone's world,
and I was humbled I added to the world.
This is why the gods made stars of mortals –
they don't take the powers of mortals,
their powers transfigured, for granted,
and lest mortals think gods can't be touched
by acts of grace, they immortalize their favorites
so to gaze at them lovingly, during their painfully long lives.
And so I make of my hearer a star also.

A man had been walking along the beach

counting the pebbles on his path

and the grains of sand sifting beneath his feet

when from the foaming sea arose, immense,

Leviathan, its crown touching the heavens.

This great serpent asked the man a favor:

to take a picture of himself, for, being so great,

he was everywhere in the world all at once

and unable to see his family, the remedy being

a photograph, so as to remember him by

when he was absent. Yet the coast, the Alps,

the sea, the continent could not contain Leviathan,

the man stepped back and back and could not frame him,

and so the beast sighed, sinking, making to leave.

And yet, to the requester, the man made a request.

And so, in the darkest abysses, the coldest seas,

underneath Leviathan's eyelids, was a photograph

of the man, so he was not alone everywhere he went.

I don't know if there is a creator,

I don't know if he lives in the wind, or if

he is tending to us patiently, even now,

or if he wove the pattern of the universe by which

all the stars and the planets came to be,

or if all of existence had to be,

if, for whatever reason, atoms must be,

life must be, and man and animal must be,

and even if we are simply thanking our origin

I would thank the phenomenon of our origin this:

he gave us thought for our sake,

not for his sake, for our sake onely,

so we're able to long for him, so we can glimmer

him, so that we're not truly alone,

wherever we are on this dusty realm,

so we can be close to him, by resembling him,

so that we can see the beauty in his world,

for wouldn't the world be pained if it weren't beautiful?

I write, sometimes, to remind myself

of the world that I have made in my mind.

And this must be why men and women wrote

even in the days without paper, even in the days

without reason, even in the days in the cell –

to remind ourselves we are here, so tenuous

this existence and its contradictions are.

And now, something that needn't be said,

or shouldn't be said, but I say anyway:

In a garden at the foot of Mount Zion was

                                Christ and his night.

With him were Peter, John and James. Late

was the hour, and heavy were their eyelids. Yet Christ

knew his time was come, and he asked them to stay awake

with him, a while. And for that first hour, only Peter

stayed with him, for he longed to understand Christ,

and at this hour he understood him not. He said,

How can it be, that you will leave us ever?

and in the night he quivered, for he was as cold

as he was born naked from his mother's womb.

To which Christ said, Peter, you would deny me

my death? Do you have so little faith

that nothing of me will last ever after?

Peter,

     why when a man cannot see, the Lord

returns him to light? why when a man begs

for bread, the Lord sees him filled? why when a woman

is shamed, the Lord makes her gravid with child?

He made all of the world, isn't all good in his eye?

Peter, the Lord says, I have made you all,

I know you all, and so suffer me a little longer.

Peter, I am the Son of God. And yet you are too.

Peter, suffer me a little longer, and as my faith

is placed in you, I know you shall do so.

Peter, under these same stars the kingdoms of earth

were offered me; and yet we were born kings,

what scepter and crown shall account us?

My father has made the body a kingdom.

My father permitted riches for some of this earth,

and, yea, I love them all; but I say unto you,

those who receive blessings after, are most blessed of all,

for never is a man too late to receive grace,

and those who suffered the Lord longest, will be ever rewarded.

Peter, you will always have the poor with you;

why, then, do you need me to stay?

Peter, you shall always be sole with yourself;

why, then, do you require more closeness with me?

And even then, he did not understand. So Christ said,

Peter, recall how the storm was exceeding strong

and how fear waxed much in your soul

234

and you believed God in his wrath would swallow you,

and by your doubtful eye and in

your passing faith you cried, Lord, if it be thou,

bid me come unto thee on the water.

And I did so, as you commanded, for I

came unto this earth to minister, not to be ministered.

Peter, even as then, if you were to call on me,

I will be with you. Peter, in spite of your faith,

when you have need of me, I will answer.

For Christ knew that no longer by fear of death

was he sore understanding. And yet Peter understood not.

Peter, verily I say unto thee, that this night

before the cock crow, thou shalt deny me thrice.

And this aroused him out of his slumber, and he cried

Lord, even if I were to die with you, you

shall never be disavowed by me. Christ then laughed.

Peter, woe unto him who betrays me, for though I

forgive him howsomever hours of the day,

he shall never forgive himself, no, not unto

the end of days will his thoughts forgive him.

Peter, when you see the crowd, exceeding wroth

so you know not what devils teem them, know

that I forgive you. Peter, I know all of you.

From the dark I knew you, unto the dark I know you.

And Christ left him a while, and thought him some,

and he doubted his death, not because it was needless,

he doubted it because he was loved much

and he loved them much more. And so he said,

Father, if you will, let this cup pass me by.

Yet, let it be as you, not I, would have it.

And when he returned to James, John and Peter,

all were fast asleep. And he said with sorrow,

Could you not abide me by the while?

The spirit is willing, but the flesh is weak.

And on that very night, as was foretold, Christ was taken,

and when his disciples saw this, they fled, and he was alone.

Before the high priest he was brought, who condemned him

to be guilty of death, and his servants did strike him.

Peter witnessed these things, and he marveled,

and he said, Wherefore are they angered?

And a maid saw him, and said of him

who he was. In his astonishment he denied

for though his body knew Christ, his soul still did not.

And this he did thrice before the cock crew,

and he recalled Christ forgave him, and he wept.

And Christ was brought before Pilate, the governor,

who asked the priests, What shall I do to him?

And they answered, We would that you crucify him.

And the governor was exceeding perplexed, for no crime

did he perceive of Christ. And he brought out Barabbas,

and asked of them, Whom of them shall I condemn?

And the people, compelled by the priests, cried, Christ,

for they knew Barabbas, and none of Christ.

And the crowd was a swirl around Christ, wroth

they smote him in the head with reeds, and spat,

and on his head they placed a crown of thorns,

calling him King of the Jews, for they themselves

were kings, in Christ's eyes. And in the throng

to each who had smote him, or spit, or mocked him,

he forgave them, for they did as to themselves,

236

so possessed by their madness they were.

And when they parted his garments, and cast lots,

he saw in them the fear of parting with their own garments,

and when they said, Save thyself, come down the cross,

he saw in them fear of their powerlessness,

and when they exhorted him, to destroy the temple,

he saw their hearts were hardened beyond believing,

and he wept. And unto them he said,

I am the Son of God, the Holy Spirit given flesh;

see, when you bleed, I bleed; when you cry,

I cry; when you are pained, I am pained;

I have made you all, I know your sufferings;

your flaws, I knew; to me, they are not;

and I love you all, I forgive you all,

and unto you shall I always abide,

even as now, even unto the dark of the grave.

And at the ninth hour, Christ cried with a loud voice,

My God, my God, why hast thou forsaken me?

For he understood then those who came before,

who also went unto their deaths, in exceeding fear,

and he grieved for them, and those too requiring

still of him, and those he loved, including himself.

Thereupon some put a sponge unto vinegar

and gave him to drink, so as to mock him.

And tasting of the vinegar, it was sweet as water,

and he knew now his time was come; he cried

with a loud voice, and gave up the ghost,

for life and death were finally as one.

And on the third day thereafter, Christ returned,

and told them this very theme, and he said,

Erect neither building nor idol to me,

for I am within all of you. On my behalf

no one onely speaks, for I speak to you all.

Let him who hears, hear. Let us tend

to the earth around us, and bestow grace

unto our brethren, and think not of the thereafter

for it shall always be there, and we are here.

But, where are you then?

                      I can tell myself this,

I can believe in all of this,

                    repeat every word,

but, Eurydice, why do you still have to die?

Even if I

          were rinsed in light,

                   my body light,

                           and my soul light too,

Why couldn't you be beside me

                    dressed in light too?

Why must I be the one who lives on?

Even after

         the stars reveal

                  their arrangements to me,

I still cry, Eurydice, don't go!

                  Come back! Eurydice!

Eurydice and I were supposed to be happy

to be alive. I just can't glimmer why

this is so impossible. We never asked for much,

indeed we lived on little, we bothered few,

we were content in our simplicity, and yet

even this fucking bareness couldn't be achieved.

Why am I supposed to hoof it alone? I'm supposed

to live on, while she has to go on content

with the few years she has been on this earth?

Am I supposed to be gratified by living,

pretending I'm privileged, while wondering every second

what it is, she would be thinking at this instant?

I just want her beside me again. I don't want

to think of her as gone, I don't want to think

of myself as having been saved, neither do I want

to think of her as having left, leaving me behind.

and I fear, if I just move on,

if I leave you behind, I lose you

forever. But, Eurydice, we haven't done enough yet.

Eurydice, I love you. It took me walking

all heaven and hell to figure it out.

And yet heaven and hell are all empty

and every world has only myself

missing you, you who were yourself only

and yourself is the only one I could love

and ever as I wander all eternity I ask,

Who else will keep Eurydice warm at night?

Who else will hold her in their arms?

Who else will give her kisses, when she deserves none?

Who else will love her as she asks to be?

And who will Eurydice love, loving her?
If true meaning comes from the meaninglessness
of meaning, if true beauty comes from the tension
of existence, then why can't beauty for me
lie in accompanying Eurydice?
But what is even the sense of that?
Why can't I just be with her?
And will I find her and love her in the next life,
or have I just lost my only chance?

If this is it, and the world is all one,
if this is it, and we are timeless beings,
if this is it, and this flesh is ornament,

Eurydice, writing is all I have of you.
This song and this night, you're with me.
Eurydice, I only ever sing about you,
and if I were to cease and these lines to stop,
how will I remember you?

Please, Eurydice, just speak to me.
...
Please, dear God,
God of all variation,
God of bottomless grace,
God of forgiveness
and truth and righteousness,
please, make this make sense to me.
...
Who is going to love me?

In whose arms will I find myself again?

And why can't they be Eurydice's?

Who else will know me

as if I didn't know myself?

...

If we're to live on the light of every word,

why, then, did you give unto me Eurydice?

why, then, did you present her to me as light

so that every drop after is dryness?

why, then, to the lightless depths

did Eurydice have to descend?

why, then, to Eurydice did you give me

to heal the sadness in her soul

then to take her and it all away?

Did you forget to take me too?

...

Is it that I'm here

to cry my last cry

and these my last years

are to bathe Eurydice in gold

and bring her back to life

on piety and piety alone?

How many cries

do you require of me?

How many wounds

must I pour

into a pitcher of pain

before it's enough?

...

I can understand everything,

241

search in the depths of meaning,
glimmer dark things in dim heart,
and find the breath of life in words,
and yet for my remaining days
I shall never understand Eurydice
as I am understood
as she deserved to be.

...

Yeah, I guess that's it. I guess
I really am talking to no one, except
myself. But I just can't let this be
my last cry, must I? If I stop
now, will my silence damn me?

...

Why can't you take me instead?
Why can't you cancel my sight
and allow Eurydice her vision?
Why couldn't I have been taken
and so I wouldn't live a long life
of cursing this world, and myself?
Why am I here, instead,
poor, crooked me?

...

Eurydice, please.
Don't descend again.
Please, don't.

...

Oh, God.

I remember my days of vinegar.

I remember my days of anger.

But none of this even matters.

Tomorrow, I know, I will descend again.

Tomorrow, you will be holding me

again. Tomorrow, I won't find you

again, for it is not mine to love again.

Yes, now I see I am the one who's dead.

Eurydice, would you come looking for me?

Aha. Ahahaha.

Hah.

A song for you

There my lover lies, in his hair moonlight,

moonlight on his face, where tears are,

streaking his face are their dried tracks,

golden, in spite of the jet night. Orpheus,

have you considered how I feel? Orpheus,

how do I stand here, knowing you cry? Orpheus,

don't you know I'm beside you? Orpheus,

don't cry anymore.

                Orpheus, I won't be with you

always, I won't wipe your tears away

every night, Orpheus, I can't say to you

every night, Be sad no more, I'm with you.

But tonight, I'm holding you.

                Orpheus,

life was a lot of little footsteps to you,

life was a lot of little kisses I gave you,

they were so little, I never felt any lesser

giving them to you, so you don't have to give back.

Orpheus, life was a lot of little distances

we closed to get to the other, and nothing

in the world negates that, and nothing

in the darkness diminishes that, and there is no

world, upon the thousands, upon the millions

and millions, that shall take these from us.

Orpheus, there shall always be this night between us,

not this wind between us, not my hands between us,

and there are no worlds in the gap separating us,

but only this night, this intimacy we share,

there are only the silences we know

and these emotions we felt,

me knowing you and you knowing me, my

weaving with you and you weaving with me,

so when the sun hides behind the horizon, sinking the earth

in shade, I'm here again, parting your hair

as you sleep, as you await the moon's rising

so that you may count the hours again until

you feel the warmth of living and loving again.

There aren't enough stars in the sky and moons

separating us from meeting again.

Orpheus, there was a time for meeting you

and there was a time for loving you, and now

there is time merely before you see me again.

And in none of this time, am I not loving you.

So cry no more, if only for my sake,

don't cry anymore, they're not for me,

I won't take them, how could I take

something so sad of yours? Orpheus,

give the night my name no longer, it doesn't

deserve it, Orpheus, don't throw curses

into the night, because sleep won't find your eyes,

nothing save your love crosses over to me,

listen, now, the song you longed to hear,

song so faint in the night, this song

separating us so short a while, this song

whereby I'm close to you, this song

of ourselves, and the love we gave

to the other and the love we made

and all that you and I are, this song

so vast because it contains all our being

and all the worlds we'll sing to the other

again, and someday soon, and all the silences

denoting the little worlds I created with you,

and still it's so short it won't last

my final words to you. Now listen,

here and forever, this song just for you,

this star, telling us we are together.